THE CHRISTMAS BOOK

Compiled by

JAMES REEVES

Illustrated by

RAYMOND BRIGGS

E. P. DUTTON & CO., INC.   :   NEW YORK

7619

For help during the preparation of this book I gratefully acknowledge my indebtedness to Miss Eve Clark and the staff of Lewes Borough Library.

J. R.

ACKNOWLEDGMENTS

Permission to use the following material is gratefully acknowledged by the Publisher:

THE CHRISTMAS ROBIN From *Try These for Size* by Janet McNeill. Reprinted by permission of Faber and Faber Ltd. and the author.

THE STONES OF PLOUHINEC From *French Legends, Tales and Fairy Stories* by Barbara Leonie Picard. Reprinted by permission of Henry Z. Walck, Inc.

THE THIEVES WHO COULDN'T HELP SNEEZING By Thomas Hardy. Reprinted by permission of the Trustees of the Estate of Thomas Hardy, Lloyd's Bank and Miss I. Cooper Willis.

CHRISTMAS UNDERGROUND From *The Wind in the Willows* by Kenneth Grahame. Reprinted by permission of Methuen & Co. Ltd.

THE OXEN From *The Collected Poems of Thomas Hardy*. Reprinted by permission of The Macmillan Company, New York.

CAROLS IN GLOUCESTERSHIRE From *The Edge of Day* by Laurie Lee. Copyright © 1959 by Laurie Lee. Reprinted by permission of William Morrow and Company, Inc.

FOR THEM and KEEPING CHRISTMAS From *A Puffin Quartet of Poets: Poems by Eleanor Farjeon*. Reprinted by permission of Penguin Books Limited.

BALLYUTILITY'S CHRISTMAS TREE From *A Pinch of Salt* by Janet McNeill. Reprinted by permission of Faber and Faber Ltd.

CHRISTMAS IS COMING From *Magic in My Pocket* by Alison Uttley. Reprinted by permission of Faber and Faber Ltd.

WAITING From *The Wandering Moon* by James Reeves. Published 1960 by E. P. Dutton & Co., Inc. and reprinted with their permission.

THE SHEPHERDS (excerpt) From *Seven Miracle Plays* by Alexander Franklin. Reprinted by permission of The Clarendon Press.

MISTLETOE, A BALLAD OF CHRISTMAS, and SNOWING By Walter de la Mare. Reprinted by permission of The Literary Trustees of Walter de la Mare and The Society of Authors as their representative.

RAGGED ROBIN (excerpt) From *Ragged Robin* by James Reeves. Copyright © 1961 by James Reeves. Reprinted by permission of E. P. Dutton & Co., Inc.

FROST From *Old Peter's Russian Tales* by Arthur Ransome. Reprinted by permission of Thomas Nelson & Sons Ltd.

CHRISTMAS From *More About Paddington* by Michael Bond. Copyright © 1959 by Michael Bond. Reprinted by permission of Houghton Mifflin Company.

MEMORIES OF CHRISTMAS From *Quite Early One Morning* by Dylan Thomas. Copyright © 1954 by New Directions Publishing Corp. All rights reserved. Reprinted by permission of New Directions Publishing Corp.

THE
CHRISTMAS
BOOK

ALSO BY JAMES REEVES

The Blackbird in the Lilac
The Peddler's Dream and Other Plays
Ragged Robin
The Story of Jackie Thimble
The Wandering Moon

Contents

Christmas

An Introduction by James Reeves

What is the first thing that comes into your mind at the sound of the word 'Christmas'? Some will say 'Presents', others 'Plenty of good food', others 'A Christmas tree'. Some will think of snow and snowmen, others of eating turkey and plum pudding on a sun-baked beach by the Pacific Ocean; some will think of parties, of pantomimes, of holly and mistletoe, of carol-singing, roasting chestnuts by a log fire.

All these things are part of Christmas, and most of them go back a very long way. But above all, Christmas means the birth of Christ, who came about two thousand years ago to bring new hope to mankind. When the angel appeared to the shepherds in the fields outside Bethlehem, he announced 'Glory to God in the highest, and on earth peace, goodwill toward men.'

But the birth of Christ is not the oldest thing associated with Christmas. The Romans had a feast called the Saturnalia, at which they also gave glory to one of their gods—Saturn. They made him sacrifices; they had feasting and games; they gave presents to the poor and the slaves; they lit torches and candles. There was no fighting. In short, 'On earth peace, goodwill toward men.' The festival of the Saturnalia was also a time when the Romans celebrated the death of the old year and the birth of the new. This was associated with what is called the winter solstice—the darkest time of the year, when days are shortest, nights longest.

During the earliest times after the beginning of Christianity the birth of Christ was not celebrated in any special way;

but later the Fathers of the Church decided to hold celebrations to mark this event. They accordingly fixed these celebrations to come annually at about the time of the winter solstice, and they took over and adapted many of the features of the Roman Saturnalia. Moreover, far from Rome—in northern Europe, for instance—there were also other festivals to mark the end of the old year, and these too had their influence on the Christian way of keeping Christmas. The festival of *Yule* comes from Scandinavia, and that of *Noël*—also originally a pre-Christian festival—from France. The Italian *Natale* once meant, not the birth of Christ, but the birth of the new year. In France and Italy the New Year has always had greater importance than Christmas Day itself.

Christmas is thought to have first come to England with Saint Augustine towards the end of the sixth century, and so has been celebrated in one form or another for nearly fourteen centuries; the efforts of the Puritans to do away with it after the Civil War in the seventeenth century were not wholly successful. In early Colonial days in America the attempts of the Puritans to spread gloom instead of rejoicing at Christmas were more successful than in the Britain of Oliver Cromwell. The religious side of Christmas has always been strongest in Catholic countries. In Italy most of the churches and many houses have their 'cribs' at the season of *Natale*—models, large or small, simple or ornate, of the stable where Christ was born, with the infant in the centre surrounded by the Holy Family, the shepherds and the farm animals.

In Britain Christmas never quite recovered from the attacks of the Puritans. It was revived with vigour after the Restoration of the monarchy, but in the eighteenth century it was not regarded as of great importance. However, it was once more revived in the early nineteenth century. The importance it has today owes much to the writer Charles Dickens and to the popular Prince Albert, husband of Queen Victoria, who brought many Christmas customs from his native Germany.

The most notable of these is the setting up of the Christmas tree, fir or spruce, in open places or indoors, illuminated by candles or electric lights and hung with gifts and ornaments. The Christmas tree was popular in America even earlier than in Britain, and its use has spread to other parts of the world where formerly it was not known.

The Christmas tree is only one of many evergreens introduced for decoration. The use of these evergreens is much older than Christianity: it was a part of the winter festivals in pagan countries to celebrate the birth of the new year by paying homage to the gods of nature who kept life going during the dark, cold season. Among these evergreens were rosemary, bays, holly, and ivy. Mistletoe is regarded by the church as unlucky because it is associated with the old pagan priests, the Druids. Holly, on the other hand, is lucky. But Britain has stuck more firmly than some countries to its old pagan practices. The custom of kissing under the mistletoe is an English one.

Ivy and bays are used in honour of the spirit of merry-making. The popularity of rosemary before Puritan times was due to its being the sign of remembrance: Christmas is the time when we remember our friends and write to them or send them presents. Some plants were believed to have magical powers. The most famous of these is the Glastonbury thorn. It was believed that Joseph of Arimathaea came to Britain with a staff which had been cut in the Holy Land. Walking up a hill in the west of England, he suddenly felt weary and full of despair. He stuck his staff into the ground and leaned upon it. Instantly it took root and blossomed. It was believed to blossom each year on Christmas Eve as a sign of the new hope which had come to the world with the birth of Christ.

One of the oldest Christmas traditions is the exchanging of presents, which was certainly a feature of the Roman Saturnalia. On the other hand Christmas cards are a comparatively modern feature, gaining popularity in England only with the introduction of the penny post in 1840. Before that time postal communication was too expensive for most people. Another feature of Christmas which is not very ancient in Britain is the Christmas cracker. This is thought to have originated in France, where children were given bags of sweets which burst when pulled in half. Later, fitted with a small explosive charge, it became increasingly popular in Victorian England.

The central point of the Christmas festival in most houses is the feast—Christmas dinner of turkey, plum pudding and mince pies. But the turkey has only come into general use fairly recently. In olden days the principal meat was the pig, which was usually killed in November when the supplies of its natural food such as acorns and beechnuts were exhausted. The boar's head, decorated with fragrant rosemary, was the centrepiece of all Christmas feasts up to the time of Elizabeth I. Towards the end of her reign, however, the turkey, sometimes known as the Indian peacock, was served instead of—or as well as—the boar's head. The turkey is thought to have been discovered by Spanish adventurers in Mexico. As a sweetmeat the heavy, rich plum pudding is peculiarly English. Other nations prefer mince pies, cakes, biscuits and gingerbread. In medieval times the chief drink was warm, spiced ale with apples in it, drunk from a wassail bowl passed from hand to hand. The word 'wassail' simply means 'Be of good health'.

Everyone knows of the 'twelve days of Christmas' from 25 December to 5 January, which in merry England, before the Puritans, were celebrated much more whole-heartedly than nowadays. Christmas Eve, now chiefly used for decorating houses and churches with evergreens and hanging up Christmas stockings, was once celebrated with games and dancing. It was also the occasion for bringing in the Yule log. This was carefully preserved from the year before and rekindled on the hearth to preserve the flame of life into the New Year. Saint Nicholas—shortened to 'Santa Claus'—long ago became the patron saint of children. In Europe he used to be thought to travel about on Christmas Eve on a horse or a donkey; the idea that he moves on an airborne sledge drawn by reindeer came from North America. The midnight Mass commemorating the birth of Christ is the central point of the religious side of Christmas. It has always been held in Catholic countries, and is becoming more and more popular throughout the Christian world. Carols and Christmas hymns were once heard far more than they are today. The earliest Christmas hymns of the medieval church were in Latin.

Boxing Day is the day on which all who have served us during the year—postmen, milkmen and tradesmen—are rewarded by gifts of money. This is an ancient custom, formerly much more in use than now. Since the nineteenth century Boxing Day has usually been the day on which pantomimes begin. With so much more entertainment, especially on the radio and television, there are signs that pantomimes are losing some of their popularity.

In some countries New Year's Eve is as important as Christmas Day. In Scotland Hogmanay, as it is called, is a time of festivity and New Year's Day a public holiday. The tradition of 'first footing' is still kept up in Britain, especially in the north. To make sure of good luck in the coming year, the first foot to cross the threshold of any house on 1 January must be that of a man—usually a dark-haired man, but in some places a fair one. The man is supposed to bring gifts of bread or cakes or a lump of coal for those living in the house. The twelfth day of Christmas is the eve of Epiphany, the day on which the three Kings from the East came to do homage and bring gifts to the new-born Saviour in Bethlehem. It was also a day for wassailing—when in the West of England cider was sprinkled on the fruit trees in order to ensure fertility during the coming year. The twelfth day was celebrated in merry England by the holding of many games, especially games of chance. Nowadays it is observed only by the taking down of all decorations. The

Christmas tree is stripped of its ornaments and put outside; holly and ivy are burnt; shelves and mantelpieces are cleared of Christmas cards, and the season is over.

Christmas is no longer what it used to be. Yet the gloom spread by the Puritans three hundred years ago has gradually been replaced by a spirit of joy, even though the season has become what is called over-commercial. The spending of money, especially in rich countries, has tended to make us forget that it is a religious as well as a pagan festival. It is different from what it was in the days of Dickens and Prince Albert; but in their time it was different from what it had been a century before them. Who knows what changes will have taken place, what old customs will have been revived a hundred years from now? Christmas is to a great extent what we make it. Its essential meaning will be always the same—'Glory to God in the highest, and on earth peace, goodwill toward men.'

The Twelve Days of Christmas
Traditional

The first day of Christmas
My true love sent to me
A partridge in a pear-tree.

The second day of Christmas
My true love sent to me
Two turtle-doves
And a partridge in a pear-tree.

The third day of Christmas
My true love sent to me
Three French hens,
Two turtle-doves
And a partridge in a pear-tree.

The fourth day of Christmas
My true love sent to me
Four colly birds,
Three French hens,
Two turtle-doves
And a partridge in a pear-tree.

The fifth day of Christmas
My true love sent to me

Five gold rings,
Four colly birds,
Three French hens,
Two turtle-doves
And a partridge in a pear-tree.

The sixth day of Christmas
My true love sent to me
Six geese a-laying,
Five gold rings,
Four colly birds,
Three French hens,
Two turtle-doves
And a partridge in a pear-tree.

The seventh day of Christmas
My true love sent to me
Seven swans a-swimming,
Six geese a-laying,
Five gold rings,
Four colly birds,
Three French hens,
Two turtle-doves
And a partridge in a pear-tree.

The eighth day of Christmas
My true love sent to me
Eight maids a-milking,
Seven swans a-swimming,
Six geese a-laying,
Five gold rings,
Four colly birds,
Three French hens,
Two turtle-doves
And a partridge in a pear-tree.

The ninth day of Christmas
My true love sent to me
Nine drummers drumming,
Eight maids a-milking,
Seven swans a-swimming,
Six geese a-laying,
Five gold rings,
Four colly birds,
Three French hens,
Two turtle doves
And a partridge in a pear-tree.

The tenth day of Christmas
My true love sent to me
Ten pipers piping,
Nine drummers drumming,
Eight maids a-milking,
Seven swans a-swimming,
Six geese a-laying,
Five gold rings,
Four colly birds,
Three French hens,
Two turtle-doves
And a partridge in a pear-tree.

The eleventh day of Christmas
My true love sent to me
Eleven ladies dancing,
Ten pipers piping,
Nine drummers drumming,
Eight maids a-milking,
Seven swans a-swimming,
Six geese a-laying,
Five gold rings,
Four colly birds,

Three French hens,
Two turtle-doves
And a partridge in a pear-tree.

The twelfth day of Christmas
My true love sent to me
Twelve lords a-leaping,
Eleven ladies dancing,
Ten pipers piping,
Nine drummers drumming,
Eight maids a-milking,
Seven swans a-swimming,
Six geese a-laying,
Five gold rings,
Four colly birds,
Three French hens,
Two turtle-doves
And a partridge in a pear-tree.

The Christmas Robin
Janet McNeill

Of all the windows in the avenue the robin likes the schoolroom window best, because the curtains are never drawn across it— in fact there are no curtains. The windows of the other houses are curtained as soon as the lights are lit inside the rooms, but since the middle of November the lights in the schoolroom are switched on about three o'clock, and they shine until the children go home, at a quarter to four.

So the robin on the window-sill gets as much schooling as

the children do, and he is a great deal more attentive than any of them are. He perches outside the pane of glass with his head set first on one side and then on the other, as each bright eye in turn scrutinizes everything that happens. He gets more than schooling. He doesn't know, of course, that he is an item on the school timetable, but he does know, and so do all the other birds in the playground and the gardens on each side of it, that every morning punctually at ten o'clock the schoolroom window is lifted and crumbs are thrown out by small eager fists. All the birds are glad to have the crumbs, especially with November hardening into December, but the robin is the only one who is glad to have the education as well.

When the children come out to play in the garden at eleven o'clock there are usually more crumbs, spilt from paper bags and out of pockets, and most of the birds sit in the bushes, ready to snatch whenever there is an opportunity. But not the robin. For he knows that the schoolmistress always opens the window while the children are outside, and she leaves it open and goes off to have coffee with the other teachers. Then the robin comes in across the window-pane, oh, very softly, to complete his education at closer quarters.

He examines the blackboard and the chalk, he looks into the inkpot and is pleased to see the reflection of his bead-bright eye looking out at him, he perches on the geography globe, but carefully, because it spins even under the weight of his little claws, he goes to see if any of the children have brought new sprays of berries for the Nature Shelf, and if they have he chooses the juiciest of them for himself, he looks critically at the handwork table and thinks that all that raffia is going to be very useful and convenient for him once the spring gets under way outside in the garden, he is sorry there are no more tadpoles to watch, circulating in the tank. And when the bell rings again and the children come stampeding into the classroom he is out through the window with a brisk lift of his wing, for he believes in punctuality as firmly as the teacher does.

Like her he is fond of neatness and tidiness, of things as they always have been, and that is why, in the first week of December, the robin was puzzled and more than a little worried. Because things in the classroom were not as they always had been—far from it! When it should have been sums it was singing, and when it should have been writing on the blackboard it was recitation, and every afternoon now seemed to have become some kind of holiday, because the desks were pushed against the wall, the chairs were set at one end of the room, and the children walked about, or knelt, or sang, in a way that they had never done before. They dressed up, too, in strange clothes that reached to their feet—even the boys in skirts—and some of the girls untwisted their pigtails and wore their hair long over their shoulders. And all the children were much more earnest and solemn than they usually were and seemed to be enjoying it in spite of themselves.

There were other changes, too. On the Monday morning that the snow began, snow dropping slowly, tantalizingly out of a grey sky, like goose-feathers, the postman brought a great many letters to the schoolmistress and she opened the envelopes and took out the coloured pictures, and set them in a row along the classroom mantelpiece.

'Christmas is coming,' she told the children, and the robin, who was paying attention, as he always did, heard what she said.

When the children went out to play—the snow had stopped as if the sky were holding its breath for a moment, and the boys and girls stamped and shouted over the thin white crust that lay on the grass—the robin went in through the window to look more closely at the pictures on the mantelpiece.

Some of them were easier to understand than others, but all of them were very interesting. There were pictures of postmen, and pictures of angels, and pictures of snowmen, too. He recognized them right away, for he had often seen postmen and snowmen and angels. And there were holly berries and fir trees, he knew about those. The fir tree at the school gate had already become important in its shawl of snow, and the holly tree blazed with berries. But there was one strange picture that frightened and perplexed him, a picture of a bird such as he had never seen.

It was a large bold bird with a large bold beak. It had eyes the size of saucers—there was no bird who had eyes like that—and legs that were much too long for it. It had—and this was the most alarming thing of all—a great red balloon of a chest, red like the red paper that now hung in loops and chains across the classroom ceiling. What a vulgar colour it was! The robin looked down at the delicate tint of his russet breast, the colour of the leaves in an autumn beech hedge, and although he was not proud he was grateful to find out how different he was from this monster.

It wasn't only the appearance of the red-chested dragon-bird that alarmed our robin—it was the thing the bird was doing. Large as any hen, it was perched on the top of a lantern—a lantern that was burning so brightly that the bird's feet must certainly have been scorched by it, if they had been an ordinary bird's feet—and in its crocodile-like beak it carried an envelope embellished ridiculously with a bow of blue ribbon. Our robin was alarmed—and puzzled—and ashamed.

There was nothing, however, to be done about it, and each morning that week, as the snow grew thicker, the postman brought more letters for the schoolmistress with pictures inside them, pictures of fir trees and holly bushes, of snowmen and angels and postmen, and another picture of this red-chested dragon-bird.

There was a little fir tree standing in a tub inside the class-room now, and the teacher had propped holly branches behind all the pictures, there were two snowmen already in the garden, there were postmen who never missed a post, there were angels if you remembered to look for them, and more at this time of year than at any other. Christmas brings all these things, the little robin said to himself, and will it bring this terrible bird as well?

One morning, for the first time since term had started in September, the window of the classroom was not opened at ten o'clock, and no crumbs were thrown out across the sill. So our robin went hungry, but there was so much that was unusual going on inside the window that he was too excited to notice. There had been no regular lessons all day. Everything was topsy-turvy and unexpected. The desks had been pushed back against the walls as soon as the children had taken off their caps and coats. The chairs were arranged in rows. Lights were lit on the fir tree—how gaily they shone! The piano played all the morning and the children sang. They dressed up, too. The little girls with long hair wore white dresses, as if they were angels. Not very good angels, the robin thought, but he knew that that was what they were.

There was a great deal, however, that he didn't understand. Early in the afternoon fathers and mothers and young sisters and brothers arrived at the school and sat on the chairs and watched and listened as the schoolchildren sang again, and the piano played. Some of the children wore crowns, and they went about their business very seriously, though the robin didn't understand what the business was.

He sat on the window-sill and saw it all. He saw as much as any of the fathers and mothers—perhaps, indeed, he saw more, because he was the only one who noticed the real angels who went past across the sky just as the children were singing. No, not the only one. One of the smallest of the school-angels noticed and waved her hand at them, but the schoolmistress, who didn't see the angels in the sky, shook her head and frowned and the school-angel didn't wave again. It was a wonderful afternoon, and went on much longer than school usually did, and after the children's singing was over there was tea for the mothers and fathers, and a great deal of talking and laughter.

There were also a great many crumbs, but they fell inside the schoolroom, and although the window was getting misty now the robin, hump-backed to keep warm, saw the crumbs and remembered how hungry he was and how long he had been sitting there. But it had been a wonderful Christmas, all that he had expected a Christmas to be, except that there was no sign at all of the red-chested dragon-bird, and for this our robin was greatly relieved.

At last the fathers and mothers with the smallest of the children took their leave, calling good-byes as they went down the path. The schoolmistress and some of the older boys and girls stayed to tidy up.

'How hot it is in here!' the schoolmistress declared, and she opened the window. She did it so suddenly that the robin was caught in the dazzle of bright noisy air.

'Look! There's a robin!' one of the children called.

He should have flown off there and then, but he was drugged and stupid with so much excitement.

'A robin! A robin!' the children called, crowding to the window.

'He's hungry,' someone suggested, and they gathered crumbs up off the scattered floor and spread them on the snow-packed sill.

'Come on, Robin.'

They were watching him, all of them—pink cheeks, bright eyes.

'Robin—Robin—come on!' they entreated.

He knew that it mattered very much to them that he should come. Gathering all his courage tightly inside his little body, he came, in a succession of rushes and pauses, quick bright glances, hesitations, determinations, panics, bravados.

'Look at his footprints in the snow! Look—oh, look!' the children called. They hung out across the sill towards him, he could feel the warmth of their excited breath.

'Hush, hush! Look at him now!'

Delicately, taking his time about it, he selected the crumbs that pleased him, eyeing them and then the children's faces, and then the crumbs again.

The children were delighted.

'Isn't he beautiful?' said the schoolmistress. 'A Christmas robin!'

A Christmas robin! So that was what he was! He was part of Christmas.

'A Christmas robin!' echoed the children.

The crumbs were eaten now. The robin flew to the laurel bush on the other side of the path and sang a carol for them, each note round and full, like a berry on a spray of winter berries.

The children clapped. Alarmed at his own bravery, our robin retreated quickly into the thickest part of the bush. and from this safe refuge he watched the window drawn down, saw the lights extinguished, heard the last of the children's footsteps, muffled in the snow, as they went down the path, heard finally the click of the gate.

Education, he pondered, was a wonderful thing. Something new to be learned every day. But from that day to this he has always wondered who was the fierce fiery-chested dragon-bird in the pictures on the mantelpiece, and he has never found out.

from *Try These For Size*

Cock-crow at Christmas
William Shakespeare

Some say that ever 'gainst that season comes
Wherein our Saviour's birth is celebrated,
The bird of dawning singeth all night long;
And then, they say, no spirit can walk abroad;
The nights are wholesome; then no planets strike,
No fairy takes, nor witch hath power to charm,
So hallow'd and so gracious is the time.

from *Hamlet*

Tomorrow Shall be my Dancing Day
Anonymous

Tomorrow shall be my dancing day:
  I would my true love did so chance
To see the legend of my play,
  To call my true love to my dance:

  Sing O my love, O my love, my love, my love;
  This have I done for my true love.

23

Then I was born of a virgin pure,
  Of her I took fleshy substánce;
Thus was I knit to man's natúre,
  To call my true love to my dance:

In a manger laid and wrapped I was,
  So very poor, this was my chance,
Betwixt an ox and a silly poor ass,
  To call my true love to my dance:

Then afterwards baptized I was;
  The Holy Ghost on me did glance,
My Father's voice heard from above,
  To call my true love·to my dance:

The Stones of Plouhinec
Barbara Leonie Picard

In parts of Brittany are found groups of the great stones known as menhirs, arranged in circles or in avenues, like tall, rough-hewn pillars. Country people will tell you that long ago they were set up by the kerions, the fairy dwarfs, and that beneath many of them the kerions hid their gold and treasure. Each group of menhirs has its own legend, and this is the story of the Stones of Plouhinec.

Near the little town of Plouhinec, close by the Breton coast, there lies a barren stretch of moor where only coarse grass grows, and the yellow broom of Brittany. On this plain stand the stones of Plouhinec, two long rows of them.

On the edge of the moor there once lived a farmer with his sister Rozennik. Rozennik was young and pretty, and she had many suitors from Plouhinec, yet she saved her smiles for Bernèz, a poor lad who worked on her brother's farm; but the farmer refused to consider Bernèz as a suitor until he could show him his pockets full of gold.

One Christmas Eve, while the farmer was feasting his men in the farmhouse kitchen, as was his yearly custom, there came a knock on the door, and outside in the cold wind stood an old beggar who asked for a meal and shelter for the night. He looked a sly, artful old rogue, and one whom it would have been unwise to trust, but because it was Christmas Eve, he was made welcome and given a bowl of soup and a place by the fire. After supper the farmer took him out to the stable and said that he might sleep there, on a pile of straw. In the stable were the ox who drew the farmer's plough and the donkey who carried to market whatever the farmer had to sell.

The beggar was just falling asleep when midnight struck, and, as everyone knows, at midnight on Christmas Eve all the beasts in a stable can speak to each other, in memory of that first Christmas in the stable at Bethlehem.

'It is a cold night,' said the donkey.

As soon as the old beggar heard the donkey speak, he pretended to be asleep and snoring, but he kept very wide awake, for it was a habit with him, whenever he could, to listen to other people talking, in case he heard something to his advantage, or else something to their disadvantage, which he might put to profitable purpose.

'No colder,' replied the ox, 'than it will be on New Year's Eve when the stones of Plouhinec go down to the river to drink and leave their treasure uncovered. Only once in every hundred years that comes to pass.' The ox looked down at the beggar, snoring on the straw. 'If this old man knew what we know, he would be off, seven nights from now, to fill his pockets from the kerions' hoard.'

'Small good would it do him,' said the donkey, 'unless he carried with him a bunch of crowsfoot and a five-leaved trefoil. Without those plants in his hand, the stones would crush him when they returned.'

'Even the crowsfoot and the five-leaved trefoil would not be enough,' said the ox, 'for, remember, whoever takes the treasure of the stones must offer in exchange a Christian soul, or the stolen treasure will turn to dust. And though a man may easily find crowsfoot, and he may, if he searches long enough, find a five-leaved trefoil, where will he find a Christian man willing to die for him?'

'That is true enough,' agreed the donkey; and the two beasts went on to talk of other matters.

But the old beggar had heard enough to make him determined to steal the treasure, and he was up and away from the farm at the first light of day, and for six days he searched all about the countryside for crowsfoot and trefoil. He found the crowsfoot soon enough, and he found trefoil, but none with more than three leaves; until on the very last day but one of the old year, he found a five-leaved trefoil. Eagerly he hurried back to Plouhinec, reaching the town on the next morning, and went at once to the moor, that he might spy out a spot to hide himself as near to the stones as possible, to be close at hand when they went, at midnight, down to the river.

But he found someone there before him. Young Bernèz had brought his midday meal of bread and cheese to eat sitting alone beneath the largest of the stones whilst he dreamt of Rozennik, and having finished his meal, he was spending the few spare minutes that remained to him before he had to return to work in idly carving a cross upon the stone by which he sat.

'What are you doing?' asked the old beggar, who recognized him as one of the men from the farmhouse where he had spent Christmas Eve.

Bernèz smiled. 'This holy sign may be of help or comfort to someone, one day. It is as good a way as any of passing an idle moment, to carve a cross on a stone.'

'That is so,' replied the beggar; but while he was speaking he was remembering the look in Bernèz' eyes as he had watched Rozennik at the feasting on Christmas Eve, for his own sharp eyes missed little, and a cunning thought came into his head. 'What would you do,' he asked, 'if you had your pockets full of gold?'

'Why,' said Bernèz, 'that is easy. I would go to the farmer and ask for Rozennik for my wife. He would not refuse me then, and I think that she would not say no to me.'

The beggar looked about him and leant his head close to Bernèz. 'I can tell you how to fill your pockets with gold, and a sack or two besides.'

'How?' asked Bernèz, surprised.

And the beggar told him what he had learnt from the ox and the ass; all save how a bunch of crowsfoot and a five-leaved trefoil were necessary if one was not to be crushed by the stones as they returned from the river, and how a Christian soul must be offered in exchange for the gold. When he had finished, Bernèz' eyes shone and he clasped the old man's hand. 'You are a good friend indeed, to tell me this and to share your good fortune with me. I will meet you here before midnight.' He finished carving his cross joyfully, and ran back to his work on the farm; whilst the beggar chuckled to himself at the thought of how easily he had found someone to die in exchange for the gold.

Before midnight they were waiting together, Bernèz and the old beggar, hidden behind a clump of broom in the darkness. No sooner had midnight struck than there was a noise as of a great thundering, the ground shook, and the huge stones heaved themselves out of the earth and began to move down to the river. 'Now,' said the beggar, 'this is the moment.' They ran forward and looked down into the pits where the stones had stood, and there, at the bottom of each pit was a heap of treasure. The beggar opened the sacks he had brought with him and began to fill them hastily, one after the other; but

Bernèz, his heart full of the thought of Rozennik, filled only his pockets with the gold.

It seemed no more than a moment later that the earth began to tremble again and the ground echoed as though to the tramp of a giant army marching. The stones, having drunk from the river, were returning to their places. Bernèz cried out in horror as he saw them loom out of the darkness. 'Quickly, quickly, or we shall be crushed to death.' But the old beggar laughed and held up his bunch of crowsfoot and his five-leaved trefoil. 'Not I,' he said, 'for I have these magic plants to protect me. But you, you are lost, and it is as well for me, since unless a Christian soul is given in exchange, my treasure will crumble away in the morning.'

With terror Bernèz heard him and saw that he had spoken the truth, for the first of the stones moved aside when it reached the beggar and his magic herbs, and after it the other stones passed on either side of him, leaving him untouched, to move close together again as they came near to Bernèz.

The young man was too afraid to try to escape. He covered his face with his hands and waited when he saw the largest stone of all bear down on him. But above the very spot where Bernèz crouched, trembling, the stone paused, and remained there, towering over him as though to protect him, while all the other stones had to move aside and so pass him by. And when Bernèz, amazed, dared to look up, he saw that the stone which sheltered him was the stone upon which he had carved a cross.

Not until all the other stones were in their places did it move, and then it went by Bernèz and on to where its own pit showed dark, with the shining treasure at the bottom. On its way it overtook the beggar, stumbling along with his heavy sacks of gold. He heard it come after him and held out the bunch of crowsfoot and the five-leaved trefoil with a triumphant shout. But because of the cross carved upon it, the magic herbs had no longer any power over the stone and it went blindly on its

way, crushing the old beggar beneath it. And so it passed on to its own place and settled into the earth again until another hundred years should have gone by. But Bernèz ran back home to the farm, as fast as his legs could carry him; and when, in the morning, he showed his pockets full of gold, the farmer did not refuse to give him his sister. And as for Rozennik, she did not say no, for she would have had him anyway, had the choice rested with her.

from French Legends, Tales and Fairy Stories

As Joseph was A-Walking
Anonymous

As Joseph was a-walking
   He heard Angels sing,
'This night shall be born
   Our Heavenly King.

'He neither shall be born
   In house nor in hall,
Nor in the place of paradise,
   But in an ox-stall.

'He shall not be clothèd
   In purple nor pall;
But all in fair linen,
   As wear babies all.

'He shall not be rockèd
   In silver nor gold,

But in a wooden cradle
   That rocks on the mould.

'He neither shall be christened
   In milk nor in wine,
But in pure spring-well water
   Fresh spring from Bethine.'

Mary took her baby,
   She dressed Him so sweet,
She laid Him in a manger,
   All there for to sleep.

As she stood over Him
   She heard Angels sing,
'Oh, bless our dear Saviour
   Our Heavenly King!'

Christmas in a Village
John Clare

Each house is swept the day before,
And windows stuck with evergreens;
The snow is besomed from the door,
And comfort crowns the cottage scenes.
Gilt holly with its thorny pricks
And yew and box with berries small,
These deck the unused candlesticks,
And pictures hanging by the wall.

Neighbours resume their annual cheer,
Wishing with smiles and spirits high
Glad Christmas and a happy year
To every morning passer-by.
Milkmaids their Christmas journeys go
Accompanied with favoured swain,
And children pace the crumping snow
To taste their granny's cake again.

Hung with the ivy's veining bough,
The ash trees round the cottage farm
Are often stripped of branches now
The cottar's Christmas hearth to warm.
He swings and twists his hazel band,
And lops them off with sharpened hook,
And oft brings ivy in his hand
To decorate the chimney nook . . .

The shepherd now no more afraid
Since custom doth the chance bestow
Starts up to kiss the giggling maid
Beneath the branch of mistletoe
That 'neath each cottage beam is seen
With pearl-like berries shining gay,
The shadow still of what hath been
Which fashion yearly fades away.

And singers too, a merry throng,
At early morn with simple skill
Yet imitate the angel's song
And chant their Christmas ditty still;
And 'mid the storm that dies and swells
By fits—in hummings softly steals
The music of the village bells
Ringing round their merry peals.

And when it's past, a merry crew
Bedecked in masks and ribbons gay,
The morris dance their sports renew
And act their winter evening play.
The clown turned king for penny praise
Storms with the actor's strut and swell,
And harlequin a laugh to raise
Wears his hunchback and tinkling bell.

And oft for pence and spicy ale
With winter nosegays pinned before,
The wassail singer tells her tale
And drawls her Christmas carols o'er,
While prentice boy with ruddy face
And rime-bepowdered dancing locks
From door to door with happy pace
Runs round to claim his Christmas box.

from *The Shepherd's Calendar*

The Thieves Who Couldn't Help Sneezing
Thomas Hardy

Many years ago, when oak trees now past their prime were
about as large as elderly gentlemen's walking-sticks, there
lived in Wessex a yeoman's son, whose name was Hubert. He
was about fourteen years of age, and was as remarkable for
his candour and lightness of heart as for his physical courage,
of which, indeed, he was a little vain.

One cold Christmas Eve his father, having no other help at

hand, sent him on an important errand to a small town several miles from home. He travelled on horseback, and was detained by the business till a late hour of the evening. At last, however, it was completed; he returned to the inn, the horse was saddled, and he started on his way. His journey homeward lay through the Vale of Blackmore, a fertile but somewhat lonely district, with heavy clay roads and crooked lanes. In those days, too, a great part of it was thickly wooded.

It must have been about nine o'clock when, riding along amid the overhanging trees upon his stout-legged cob, Jerry, and singing a Christmas carol, to be in harmony with the season, Hubert fancied that he heard a noise among the boughs. This recalled to his mind that the spot he was traversing bore an evil name. Men had been waylaid there. He looked at Jerry, and wished he had been of any other colour than light grey; for on this account the docile animal's form was visible even here in the dense shade. 'What do I care?' he said aloud, after a few minutes of reflection. 'Jerry's legs are too nimble to allow any highwayman to come near me.'

'Ha! ha! indeed,' was said in a deep voice; and the next moment a man darted from the thicket on his right hand, another man from the thicket on his left hand, and another from a tree-trunk a few yards ahead. Hubert's bridle was seized, he was pulled from his horse, and although he struck out with all his might, as a brave boy would naturally do, he was overpowered. His arms were tied behind him, his legs bound tightly together, and he was thrown into a ditch. The robbers, whose faces he could now dimly perceive to be artificially blackened, at once departed, leading off the horse.

As soon as Hubert had a little recovered himself, he found that by great exertion he was able to extricate his legs from the cord; but, in spite of every endeavour, his arms remained bound as fast as before. All, therefore, that he could do was to rise to his feet and proceed on his way with his arms behind him, and trust to chance for getting them unfastened. He knew that it would be impossible to reach home on foot that night, and in such a condition; but he walked on. Owing to the confusion which this attack caused in his brain, he lost his way, and would have been inclined to lie down and rest till morning among the dead leaves had he not known the danger of sleeping without wrappers in a frost so severe. So he wandered farther onwards, his arms wrung and numbed by the cord which pinioned him, and his heart aching for the loss of poor Jerry, who never had been known to kick, or bite, or show a single vicious habit. He was not a little glad when he discerned through the trees a distant light. Towards this he made his way, and presently found himself in front of a large mansion with flanking wings, gables, and towers, the battlements and chimneys showing their shapes against the stars.

All was silent; but the door stood wide open, it being from this door that the light shone which had attracted him. On entering he found himself in a vast apartment arranged as a dining-hall, and brilliantly illuminated. The walls were covered with a great deal of dark wainscoting, formed into moulded panels, carvings, closet-doors, and the usual fittings of a house of that kind. But what drew his attention most was the large table in the midst of the hall, upon which was spread a sumptuous supper, as yet untouched. Chairs were placed around, and it appeared as if something had occurred to interrupt the meal just at the time when all were ready to begin.

Even had Hubert been so inclined, he could not have eaten in his helpless state, unless by dipping his mouth into the dishes, like a pig or cow. He wished first to obtain assistance; and was about to penetrate farther into the house for that purpose when he heard hasty footsteps in the porch and the words, 'Be quick!' uttered in the deep voice which had reached him when he was dragged from the horse. There was only just time for him to dart under the table before three men entered the dining-hall. Peeping from beneath the hanging edges of the tablecloth, he perceived that their faces, too, were blackened,

which at once removed any doubts he may have felt that these were the same thieves.

'Now, then,' said the first—the man with the deep voice—'let us hide ourselves. They will all be back again in a minute. That was a good trick to get them out of the house—eh?'

'Yes. You well imitated the cries of a man in distress,' said the second.

'Excellently,' said the third.

'But they will soon find out that it was a false alarm. Come, where shall we hide? It must be some place we can stay in for two or three hours, till all are in bed and asleep. Ah! I have it. Come this way! I have learnt that the farther cupboard is not opened once in a twelve-month; it will serve our purpose exactly.'

The speaker advanced into a corridor which led from the hall. Creeping a little farther forward, Hubert could discern that the cupboard stood at the end, facing the dining-hall. The thieves entered it, and closed the door. Hardly breathing, Hubert glided forward, to learn a little more of their intention, if possible; and, coming close, he could hear the robbers whispering about the different rooms where the jewels, plate, and other valuables of the house were kept, which they plainly meant to steal.

They had not been long in hiding when a gay chattering of ladies and gentlemen was audible on the terrace without. Hubert felt that it would not do to be caught prowling about the house, unless he wished to be taken for a robber himself, and stood in a dark corner of the porch, where he could see everything without being himself seen. In a moment or two a whole troop of personages came gliding past him into the house. There were an elderly gentleman and lady, eight or nine young ladies, as many young men, besides half a dozen menservants and maids. The mansion had apparently been quite emptied of its occupants.

'Now, children and young people, we will resume our

meal,' said the old gentleman. 'What the noise could have been I cannot understand. I never felt so certain in my life that there was a person being murdered outside my door.'

Then the ladies began saying how frightened they had been, and how they had expected an adventure, and how it had ended in nothing after all.

'Wait a while,' said Hubert to himself. 'You'll have adventure enough by-and-by, ladies.'

It appeared that the young men and women were married sons and daughters of the old couple, who had come that day to spend Christmas with their parents.

The door was then closed, Hubert being left outside in the porch. He thought this a proper moment for asking their assistance; and, since he was unable to knock with his hands, began boldly to kick the door.

'Hullo! What disturbance are you making here?' said a footman who opened it; and, seizing Hubert by the shoulder, he pulled him into the dining-hall. 'Here's a strange boy I have found making a noise in the porch, Sir Simon.'

Everybody turned.

'Bring him forward,' said Sir Simon, the old gentleman before mentioned. 'What were you doing there, my boy?'

'Why, his arms are tied!' said one of the ladies.

'Poor fellow!' said another.

Hubert at once began to explain that he had been waylaid on his journey home, robbed of his horse, and mercilessly left in this condition by the thieves.

'Only to think of it!' exclaimed Sir Simon.

'That's a likely story,' said one of the gentlemen-guests, incredulously.

'Doubtful, hey?' asked Sir Simon.

'Perhaps he's a robber himself,' suggested a lady.

'There is a curiously wild wicked look about him, certainly, now that I examine him closely,' said the old mother.

Hubert blushed with shame; and, instead of continuing

his story, and relating that robbers were concealed in the house, he doggedly held his tongue, and half resolved to let them find out their danger for themselves.

'Well, untie him,' said Sir Simon. 'Come, since it is Christmas Eve, we'll treat him well. Here, my lad; sit down in that empty seat at the bottom of the table, and make as good a meal as you can. When you have had your fill we will listen to more particulars of your story.'

The feast then proceeded; and Hubert, now at liberty, was not at all sorry to join in. The more they ate and drank the merrier did the company become; the wine flowed freely, the logs flared up the chimney, the ladies laughed at the gentlemen's stories; in short, all went as noisily and as happily as a Christmas gathering in old times possibly could do.

Hubert, in spite of his hurt feelings at their doubts of his honesty, could not help being warmed both in mind and in body by the good cheer, the scene, and the example of hilarity set by his neighbours. At last he laughed as heartily at their stories and repartees as the old Baronet, Sir Simon, himself. When the meal was almost over one of the sons, who had drunk a little too much wine, after the manner of men in that century, said to Hubert, 'Well, my boy, how are you? Can you take a pinch of snuff?' He held out one of the snuff-boxes which were then becoming common among young and old throughout the country.

'Thank you,' said Hubert, accepting a pinch.

'Tell the ladies who you are, what you are made of, and what you can do,' the young man continued, slapping Hubert upon the shoulder.

'Certainly,' said our hero, drawing himself up, and thinking it best to put a bold face on the matter. 'I am a travelling magician.'

'Indeed!'

'What shall we hear next?'

'Can you call up spirits from the vasty deep, young wizard?'

'I can conjure up a tempest in a cupboard,' Hubert replied.

'Ha-ha!' said the old Baronet, pleasantly rubbing his hands. 'We must see this performance. Girls, don't go away: here's something to be seen.'

'Not dangerous, I hope?' said the old lady.

Hubert rose from the table. 'Hand me your snuff-box, please,' he said to the young man who had made free with him. 'And now,' he continued, 'without the least noise, follow me. If any of you speak it will break the spell.'

They promised obedience. He entered the corridor, and, taking off his shoes, went on tiptoe to the cupboard door, the guests advancing in a silent group at a little distance behind him. Hubert next placed a stool in front of the door, and, by standing upon it, was tall enough to reach the top. He then, just as noiselessly, poured all the snuff from the box along the upper edge of the door, and, with a few short puffs of breath, blew the snuff through the chink into the interior of the cupboard. He held up his finger to the assembly, that they might be silent.

'Dear me, what's that?' said the old lady, after a minute or two had elapsed.

A suppressed sneeze had come from inside the cupboard.

Hubert held up his finger again.

'How very singular,' whispered Sir Simon. 'This is most interesting.'

Hubert took advantage of the moment to gently slide the bolt of the cupboard door into its place. 'More snuff,' he said, calmly.

'More snuff,' said Sir Simon. Two or three gentlemen passed their boxes, and the contents were blown in at the top of the cupboard. Another sneeze, not quite so well suppressed as the first, was heard: then another, which seemed to say that it would not be suppressed under any circumstances whatever. At length there arose a perfect storm of sneezes.

'Excellent, excellent for one so young!' said Sir Simon. 'I am much interested in this trick of throwing the voice—called, I believe, ventriloquism.'

'More snuff,' said Hubert.

'More snuff,' said Sir Simon. Sir Simon's man brought a large jar of the best scented Scotch.

Hubert once more charged the upper chink of the cupboard, and blew the snuff into the interior, as before. Again he charged, and again, emptying the whole contents of the jar. The tumult of sneezes became really extraordinary to listen to—there was no cessation. It was like wind, rain, and sea battling in a hurricane.

'I believe there are men inside, and that it is no trick at all!' exclaimed Sir Simon, the truth flashing on him.

'There are,' said Hubert. 'They are come to rob the house; and they are the same who stole my horse.'

The sneezes changed to spasmodic groans. One of the thieves, hearing Hubert's voice, cried, 'Oh! mercy! mercy! let us out of this!'

'Where's my horse?' cried Hubert.

'Tied to the tree in the hollow behind Short's Gibbet. Mercy! mercy! let us out, or we shall die of suffocation!'

All the Christmas guests now perceived that this was no longer sport, but serious earnest. Guns and cudgels were procured; all the menservants were called in, and arranged in position outside the cupboard. At a signal Hubert withdrew the bolt, and stood on the defensive. But the three robbers, far from attacking them, were found crouching in the corner, gasping for breath. They made no resistance; and, being pinioned, were placed in an outhouse till the morning.

Hubert now gave the remainder of his story to the assembled company, and was profusely thanked for the services he had rendered. Sir Simon pressed him to stay over the night, and accept the use of the best bedroom the house afforded, which had been occupied by Queen Elizabeth and King Charles successively when on their visits to this part of the country. But

Hubert declined, being anxious to find his horse Jerry, and to test the truth of the robbers' statements concerning him.

Several of the guests accompanied Hubert to the spot behind the gibbet, alluded to by the thieves as where Jerry was hidden. When they reached the knoll and looked over, behold! there the horse stood, uninjured, and quite unconcerned. At sight of Hubert he neighed joyfully: and nothing could exceed Hubert's gladness at finding him. He mounted, wished his friends 'Good night!' and cantered off in the direction they pointed out, reaching home safely about four o'clock in the morning.

Christmas Eve
Anonymous

Whosoever on ye nighte of ye nativity of ye yonge Lord Jesus, in ye greate snows, shall fare forth bearing a succulent bone for ye lost and lamenting hounde, a whisp of hay for ye shivering horse, a cloak of warm raiment for ye stranded wayfarer, a garland of bright berries for one who has worn chains, a dish of crumbs for all huddled birds who thought that song was dead, and divers lush sweetmeats for such babes' faces as peer from lonely windows:

To him shall be proffered and returned gifts of such an astonishment as will rival the hues of the peacock, and the harmonies of heaven, so that though he live to ye greate age when man goes stooping and querulous because of the nothing that is left in him, yet shall he walk upright and remembering, as one whose hearte shines like a greate star in his breaste.

A Very Great Curiosity

Readers of *The Newcastle Chronicle* for 6 January 1770 must
have been amused by this story:

Monday last was brought from Howick to Berwick, to be
shipp'd for London, for Sir Hen. Grey, Bart., a pie, the contents whereof are as follows: viz. 2 bushels of flour, 20 lb of
butter, 4 geese, 2 turkeys, 2 rabbits, 4 wild ducks, 2 woodcocks,
6 snipes, and 4 partridges; 2 neats' tongues, 2 curlews, 7 blackbirds, and 6 pigeons: it is supposed a very great curiosity was
made by Mrs Dorothy Patterson, housekeeper at Howick. It
was near nine feet in circumference at bottom, weighs about
twelve stones, will take two men to present it to table; it is
neatly fitted with a case, and four small wheels to facilitate its
use to every guest that inclines to partake of its contents at
table.

The Holly and the Ivy
Traditional

The holly and the ivy,
When they are both full grown,
Of all the trees that are in the wood,
The holly bears the crown:

The rising of the sun
And the running of the deer,
The playing of the merry organ,
Sweet singing in the choir.

The holly bears a blossom,
As white as the lily flower,
And Mary bore sweet Jesus Christ,
To be our sweet Saviour:

The holly bears a berry,
As red as any blood,
And Mary bore sweet Jesus Christ
To do poor sinners good:

The holly bears a prickle,
As sharp as any thorn,
And Mary bore sweet Jesus Christ
On Christmas day in the morn:

45

The holly bears a bark,
As bitter as any gall,
And Mary bore sweet Jesus Christ
For to redeem us all:

The holly and the ivy,
When they are both full grown,
Of all the trees that are in the wood,
The holly bears the crown.

Christmas Underground
Kenneth Grahame

'What a capital little house this is!' Mr Rat called out cheerily.
'So compact! So well planned! Everything here and everything in its place! We'll make a jolly night of it. The first
thing we want is a good fire; I'll see to that—I always know
where to find things. So this is the parlour? Splendid! Your own
idea, those little sleeping-bunks in the wall? Capital! Now, I'll
fetch the wood and the coals, and you get a duster, Mole—
you'll find one in the drawer of the kitchen table—and try
and smarten things up a bit. Bustle about, old chap!'

Encouraged by his inspiriting companion, the Mole roused
himself and dusted and polished with energy and heartiness,
while the Rat, running to and fro with armfuls of fuel, soon
had a cheerful blaze roaring up the chimney. He hailed the
Mole to come and warm himself; but Mole promptly had
another fit of the blues, dropping down on a couch in dark
despair and burying his face in his duster.

'Rat,' he moaned, 'how about your supper, you poor, cold, hungry, weary animal? I've nothing to give you—nothing— not a crumb!'

'What a fellow you are for giving in!' said the Rat reproach- fully. 'Why, only just now I saw a sardine-opener on the kitchen dresser, quite distinctly; and everybody knows that means there are sardines about somewhere in the neighbourhood. Rouse yourself! pull yourself together, and come with me and forage.'

They went and foraged accordingly, hunting through every cupboard and turning out every drawer. The result was not so very depressing after all, though of course it might have been better; a tin of sardines—a box of captain's biscuits, nearly full—and a German sausage encased in silver paper.

'There's a banquet for you!' observed the Rat, as he arranged the table. 'I know some animals who would give their ears to be sitting down to supper with us tonight!'

'No bread!' groaned the Mole dolorously; 'no butter, no—'

'No *pâté de foie gras*, no champagne!' continued the Rat, grinning. 'And that reminds me—what's that little door at the end of the passage? Your cellar, of course! Every luxury in this house! Just you wait a minute.'

He made for the cellar door, and presently re-appeared, somewhat dusty, with a bottle of beer in each paw and another under each arm. 'Self-indulgent beggar you seem to be, Mole,' he observed. 'Deny yourself nothing. This is really the jolliest little place I ever was in. Now, wherever did you pick up those prints? Make the place look so home-like, they do. No wonder you're so fond of it, Mole. Tell us all about it, and how you came to make it what it is.'

Then, while the Rat busied himself fetching plates, and knives and forks, and mustard which he mixed in an egg-cup, the Mole, his bosom still heaving with the stress of his recent emotion, related—somewhat shyly at first, but with more free- dom as he warmed to his subject—how this was planned, and how that was thought out, and how this was got through a windfall from an aunt, and that was a wonderful find and a bargain, and this other thing was bought out of laborious savings and a certain amount of 'going without'. His spirits finally quite restored, he must needs go and caress his possessions, and take a lamp and show off their points to his visitor, and expatiate on them, quite forgetful of the supper they both so much needed; Rat, who was desperately hungry but strove to conceal it, nodding seriously, examining with a puckered brow, and saying, 'Wonderful', and 'Most remarkable', at intervals, when the chance for an observation was given him.

At last the Rat succeeded in decoying him to the table, and had just got seriously to work with the sardine-opener when sounds were heard from the forecourt without—sounds like the scuffling of small feet in the gravel and a confused murmur of tiny voices, while broken sentences reached them—'Now, all in a line—hold the lantern up a bit, Tommy—clear your throats first—no coughing after I say one, two, three.— Where's young Bill?—Here, come on, do, we're all a-waiting—'

'What's up?' inquired the Rat, pausing in his labours.

'I think it must be the field-mice,' replied the Mole, with a touch of pride in his manner. 'They go round carol-singing regularly at this time of the year. They're quite an institution in these parts. And they never pass me over—they come to Mole End last of all; and I used to give them hot drinks, and supper sometimes, when I could afford it. It will be like old times to hear them again.'

'Let's have a look at them!' cried the Rat, jumping up and running to the door.

It was a pretty sight, and a seasonable one, that met their eyes when they flung the door open. In the forecourt, lit by the dim rays of a horn lantern, some eight or ten little field-mice stood in a semi-circle, red worsted comforters round their throats, their forepaws thrust deep into their pockets, their feet jigging for warmth. With bright beady eyes they glanced shyly at each other, sniggering a little, sniffing and applying coat-sleeves a good deal. As the door opened, one of the elder ones that carried the lantern was just saying, 'Now then, one, two, three!' and forthwith their shrill little voices uprose on the air, singing one of the old-time carols that their forefathers composed in fields that were fallow and held by frost, or when snow-bound in chimney corners, and handed down to be sung in the miry street to lamp-lit windows at Yule-time.

Villagers all, this frosty tide,
Let your doors swing open wide,
Though wind may follow, and snow beside,
Yet draw us in by your fire to bide;
    Joy shall be yours in the morning!

Here we stand in the cold and the sleet,
Blowing fingers and stamping feet,
Come from far away you to greet—
You by the fire and we in the street—
    Bidding you joy in the morning!

For ere one half of the night was gone,
Sudden a star has led us on,
Raining bliss and benison—
Bliss tomorrow and more anon,
    Joy for every morning!

Goodman Joseph toiled through the snow—
Saw the star o'er a stable low;
Mary she might not further go—
Welcome thatch, and litter below!
    Joy was hers in the morning!

And when they heard the angels tell
'Who were the first to cry Nowell?

Animals all, as it befell,
In the stable where they did dwell!
Joy shall be theirs in the morning!'

The voices ceased, the singers, bashful but smiling, exchanged sidelong glances, and silence succeeded—but for a moment only. Then, from up above and far away, down the tunnel they had so lately travelled was borne to their ears in a faint musical hum the sound of distant bells ringing a joyful and clangorous peal.

'Very well sung, boys!' cried the Rat heartily. 'And now come along in, all of you, and warm yourselves by the fire, and have something hot!'

'Yes, come along, field-mice,' cried the Mole eagerly. 'This is quite like old times! Shut the door after you. Pull up that settle to the fire. Now, you just wait a minute, while we—O, Ratty!' he cried in despair, plumping down on a seat, with tears impending. 'Whatever are we doing? We've nothing to give them!'

'You leave all that to me,' said the masterful Rat. 'Here, you with the lantern! Come over this way. I want to talk to you. Now, tell me, are there any shops open at this hour of the night?'

'Why, certainly, sir,' replied the field-mouse respectfully. 'At this time of the year our shops keep open to all sorts of hours.'

'Then look here!' said the Rat. 'You go off at once, you and your lantern, and you get me—'

Here much muttered conversation ensued, and the Mole only heard bits of it, such as—'Fresh, mind!—no, a pound of that will do—see you get Buggins's, for I won't have any other —no, only the best—if you can't get it there, try somewhere else—yes, of course, home-made, no tinned stuff—well then, do the best you can!' Finally, there was a chink of coin passing from paw to paw, the field-mouse was provided with an ample

basket for his purchases, and off he hurried, he and his lantern.

The rest of the field-mice, perched in a row on the settle, their small legs swinging, gave themselves up to the enjoyment of the fire, and toasted their chilblains till they tingled; while the Mole, failing to draw them into easy conversation, plunged into family history and made each of them recite the names of his numerous brothers, who were too young, it appeared, to be allowed to go out a-carolling this year, but looked forward very shortly to winning the parental consent.

The Rat, meanwhile, was busy examining the label on one of the beer-bottles. 'I perceive this to be Old Burton,' he remarked approvingly. '*Sensible* Mole! The very thing! Now we shall be able to mull some ale! Get the things ready, Mole, while I draw the corks.'

It did not take long to prepare the brew and thrust the tin heater well into the red heart of the fire; and soon every field-mouse was sipping and coughing and choking (for a little mulled ale goes a long way) and wiping his eyes and laughing and forgetting he had ever been cold in all his life.

'They act plays too, these fellows,' the Mole explained to the Rat. 'Make them up all by themselves, and act them after-wards. And very well they do it, too! They gave us a capital one last year, about a field-mouse who was captured at sea by a Barbary corsair, and made to row in a galley; and when he escaped and got home again, his lady-love had gone into a convent. Here, *you*! You were in it, I remember. Get up and recite a bit.'

The field-mouse addressed got up on his legs, giggled shyly, looked round the room, and remained absolutely tongue-tied. His comrades cheered him on, Mole coaxed and encouraged him, and the Rat went so far as to take him by the shoulders and shake him; but nothing could overcome his stage-fright. They were all busily engaged on him like watermen applying the Royal Humane Society's regulations to a case of long submersion, when the latch clicked, the door opened, and the field-mouse with the lantern re-appeared, staggering under the weight of his basket.

There was no more talk of play-acting once the very real and solid contents of the basket had been tumbled out on the table. Under the generalship of Rat, everybody was set to do something or to fetch something. In a very few minutes supper was ready, and Mole, as he took the head of the table in a sort of dream, saw a lately barren board set thick with savoury comforts; saw his little friends' faces brighten and beam as they fell to without delay; and then let himself loose—for he was famished indeed—on the provender so magically provided, thinking what a happy home-coming this had turned out, after all. As they ate, they talked of old times, and the field-mice gave him the local gossip up to date, and answered as well as they could the hundred questions he had to ask them. The Rat said little or nothing, only taking care that each guest had what he wanted, and plenty of it, and that Mole had no trouble or anxiety about anything.

They clattered off at last, very grateful and showering wishes of the season, with their jacket pockets stuffed with remembrances for the small brothers and sisters at home. When the door had closed on the last of them and the chink of the lanterns had died away, Mole and Rat kicked the fire up, drew their chairs in, brewed themselves a last nightcap of mulled ale, and discussed the events of the long day. At last the Rat, with a tremendous yawn, said, 'Mole, old chap, I'm ready to drop. Sleepy is simply not the word. That your own bunk over on that side? Very well, then, I'll take this. What a ripping little house this is! Everything so handy!'

He clambered into his bunk and rolled himself well up in the blankets, and slumber gathered him forthwith, as a swath of barley is folded into the arms of the reaping-machine.

The weary Mole also was glad to turn in without delay, and soon had his head on his pillow, in great joy and contentment. But ere he closed his eyes he let them wander round his old room, mellow in the glow of the firelight that played or rested on familiar and friendly things which had long been un-consciously a part of him, and now smilingly received him back, without rancour. He was now in just the frame of mind that the tactful Rat had quietly worked to bring about in him. He saw clearly how plain and simple—how narrow, even—it all was; but clearly, too, how much it all meant to him, and the special value of some such anchorage in one's existence. He did not at all want to abandon the new life and its splendid spaces, to turn his back on sun and air and all they offered him and creep home and stay there; the upper world was all too strong, it called to him still, even down there, and he knew he must return to the larger stage. But it was good to think he had this to come back to, this place which was all his own, these

things which were so glad to see him again and could always
be counted upon for the same simple welcome.

from Wind in the Willows

The Oxen
Thomas Hardy

Christmas Eve, and twelve of the clock.
  'Now they are all on their knees,'
An elder said as we sat in a flock
  By the embers in hearthside ease.

We pictured the meek mild creatures where
  They dwelt in their strawy pen,

Nor did it occur to one of us there
  To doubt they were kneeling then.

So fair a fancy few would weave
  In these years! Yet, I feel,
If someone said on Christmas Eve,
  'Come; see the oxen kneel

'In the lonely barton by yonder coomb
  Our childhood used to know,'
I should go with him in the gloom,
  Hoping it might be so.

The Night before Christmas
Clement C. Moore

'Twas the night before Christmas, when all through the house
Not a creature was stirring, not even a mouse;
The stockings were hung by the chimney with care,
In hopes that St Nicholas soon would be there;
The children were nestled all snug in their beds,
While visions of sugarplums danced in their heads;

And Mamma in her 'kerchief, and I in my cap,
Had just settled our brains for a long winter's nap;
When out on the lawn there arose such a clatter,
I sprang from the bed to see what was the matter.
Away to the window I flew like a flash,
Tore open the shutters and threw up the sash.

The moon, on the breast of the new-fallen snow,
Gave the lustre of midday to objects below,
When what to my wondering eyes should appear,
But a miniature sleigh, and eight tiny reindeer,
With a little old driver, so lively and quick,
I knew in a moment it must be St Nick.

More rapid than eagles his coursers they came,
And he whistled and shouted, and called them by name;
'Now, Dasher! Now, Dancer! Now, Prancer and Vixen!
On, Comet! On, Cupid! On, Donner and Blitzen!
To the top of the porch! To the top of the wall!
Now, dash away! Dash away! Dash away all!'

As dry leaves that before the wild hurricane fly,
When they meet with an obstacle, mount to the sky;
So up to the housetop the coursers they flew,
With the sleigh full of toys, and St Nicholas, too.

And then, in a twinkling, I heard on the roof
The prancing and pawing of each little hoof—
As I drew in my head, and was turning around,
Down the chimney St Nicholas came with a bound.

He was dressed all in fur, from his head to his foot,
And his clothes were all tarnished with ashes and soot;
A bundle of toys he had flung on his back,
And he looked like a pedlar just opening his pack.
His eyes—how they twinkled! His dimples, how merry!
His cheeks were like roses, his nose like a cherry!

His droll little mouth was drawn up like a bow,
And the beard of his chin was as white as the snow;
The stump of a pipe he held tight in his teeth,
And the smoke it encircled his head like a wreath;

He had a broad face and a little round belly
That shook, when he laughed, like a bowl full of jelly.

He was chubby and plump, a right jolly old elf,
And I laughed, when I saw him, in spite of myself;
A wink of his eye and a twist of his head,
Soon gave me to know I had nothing to dread;
He spoke not a word, but went straight to his work,
And filled all the stockings; then turned with a jerk,

And laying his finger aside of his nose,
And giving a nod, up the chimney he rose;
He sprang to his sleigh, to his team gave a whistle,
And away they all flew like the down of a thistle.
But I heard him exclaim, ere he drove out of sight,
'Happy Christmas to all, and to all a good night.'

Carols in Gloucestershire
Laurie Lee

Later, towards Christmas, there was heavy snow, which raised
the roads to the top of the hedges. There were millions of
tons of the lovely stuff, plastic, pure, all-purpose, which nobody
owned, which one could carve or tunnel, eat, or just throw
about. It covered the hills and cut off the villages, but nobody
thought of rescues; for there was hay in the barns and flour in
the kitchens, the women baked bread, the cattle were fed and
sheltered—we'd been cut off before, after all.

The week before Christmas, when snow seemed to lie

thickest, was the moment for carol-singing; and when I think back to those nights it is to the crunch of snow and to the lights of the lanterns on it. Carol-singing in my village was a special tithe for the boys, the girls had little to do with it. Like hay-making, black-berrying, stone-clearing and wishing-people-a-happy-Easter, it was one of our seasonal perks.

By instinct we knew just when to begin it; a day too soon and we should have been unwelcome, a day too late and we should have received lean looks from people whose bounty was already exhausted. When the true moment came, exactly balanced, we recognized it and were ready.

So as soon as the wood had been stacked in the oven to dry for the morning fire, we put on our scarves and went out through the streets, calling loudly between our hands, till the various boys who knew the signal ran out from their houses to join us.

One by one they came stumbling over the snow, swinging their lanterns around their heads, shouting and coughing horribly.

'Coming carol-barking then?'

We were the Church Choir, so no answer was necessary. For a year we had praised the Lord out of key, and as a reward for this service—on top of the Outing—we now had the right to visit all the big houses, to sing our carols and collect our tribute.

To work them all in meant a five-mile journey over wild and generally snowed-up country. So the first thing we did was to plan our route; a formality, as the route never changed. All the same, we blew on our fingers and argued; and then we chose our Leader. This was not binding, for we all fancied ourselves as Leaders, and he who started the night in that position usually trailed home with a bloody nose.

Eight of us set out that night. There was Sixpence the Simple, who had never sung in his life (he just worked his mouth in Church); the brothers Horace and Boney, who were always

fighting everybody and always getting the worst of it; Clergy Green, the preaching maniac; Walt the bully, and my two brothers. As we went down the lane other boys, from other villages, were already about the hills, bawling 'Kingwenslush', and shouting through keyholes 'Knock on the knocker! Ring at the Bell! Give us a penny for singing so well!' They weren't an approved charity as we were, the Choir; but competition was in the air.

Our first call as usual was the house of the Squire, and we trouped nervously down his drive. For light we had candles in marmalade-jars suspended on loops of string, and they threw pale gleams on the towering snowdrifts that stood on each side of the drive. A blizzard was blowing, but we were well wrapped up, with Army puttees on our legs, woollen hats on our heads, and several scarves around our ears.

As we approached the Big House across its white silent lawns, we too grew respectfully silent. The lake near by was stiff and black, the waterfall frozen and still. We arranged ourselves shuffling around the big front door, then knocked and announced the Choir.

A maid bore the tidings of our arrival away into the echoing distances of the house, and while we waited we cleared our throats noisily. Then she came back, and the door was left ajar for us, and we were bidden to begin. We brought no music, the carols were in our heads. 'Let's give 'em "Wild Shepherds",' said Jack. We began in confusion, plunging into a wreckage of keys, of different words and tempo; but we gathered our strength; he who sang loudest took the rest of us with him, and the carol took shape if not sweetness.

This huge stone house, with its ivied walls, was always a mystery to us. What were those gables, those rooms and attics, those narrow windows veiled by the cedar trees? As we sang 'Wild Shepherds' we craned our necks, gaping into that lamp-lit hall which we had never entered; staring at the muskets and untenanted chairs, the great tapestries furred by dust —until suddenly, on the stairs, we saw the old Squire himself standing and listening with his head on one side.

He didn't move until we'd finished; then slowly he tottered towards us, dropped two coins in our box with a trembling hand, scratched his name in the book we carried, gave us each a long look with his moist blind eyes, then turned away in silence.

As though released from a spell, we took a few sedate steps, then broke into a run for the gate. We didn't stop till we were out of the grounds. Impatient, at last, to discover the extent of his bounty, we squatted by the cowsheds, held our lanterns over the book, and saw that he had written 'Two Shillings'. This was quite a good start. No one of any worth in the district would dare to give us less than the Squire.

So with money in the box, we pushed on up the valley, pouring scorn on each other's performance. Confident now, we began to consider our quality and whether one carol was not better suited to us than another. Horace, Walt said, shouldn't sing at all; his voice was beginning to break. Horace disputed this and there was a brief token battle—they fought as they walked, kicking up divots of snow, then they forgot it, and Horace still sang.

Steadily we worked through the length of the valley, going from house to house, visiting the lesser and the greater gentry— the farmers, the doctors, the merchants, the majors and other exalted persons. It was freezing hard and blowing too; yet not for a moment did we feel the cold. The snow blew into our faces, into our eyes and mouths, soaked through our puttees, got into our boots, and dripped from our woollen caps. But we did not care. The collecting-box grew heavier, and the list of names in the book longer and more extravagant, each trying to outdo the other.

Mile after mile we went, fighting against the wind, falling into snowdrifts, and navigating by the lights of the houses. And yet we never saw our audience. We called at house after house;

we sang in courtyards and porches, outside windows, or in the damp gloom of hallways; we heard voices from hidden rooms; we smelt rich clothes and strange hot food; we saw maids bearing in dishes or carrying away coffee-cups; we received nuts, cakes, figs, preserved ginger, dates, cough-drops and money; but we never once saw our patrons. We sang as it were at the castle walls, and apart from the Squire, who had shown himself to prove that he was still alive, we never expected it otherwise.

As the night drew on there was trouble with Boney. 'Noël', for instance, had a rousing harmony which Boney persisted in singing, and singing flat. The others forbade him to sing it at all, and Boney said he would fight us. Picking himself up, he agreed we were right, then he disappeared altogether. He just turned away and walked into the snow and wouldn't answer when we called him back. Much later, as we reached a far point up the valley, somebody said 'Hark!' and we stopped to listen. Far away across the fields from the distant village came the sound of a frail voice singing, singing 'Noël', and singing it flat—it was Boney, branching out on his own.

We approached our last house high up on the hill, the place of Joseph the farmer. For him we had chosen a special carol, which was about the other Joseph, so that we always felt that singing it added a spicy cheek to the night. The last stretch of country to reach his farm was perhaps the most difficult of all. In these rough bare lanes, open to all winds, sheep were buried and wagons lost. Huddled together, we tramped in one another's footsteps, powdered snow blew into our screwed-up eyes, the candles burnt low, some blew out altogether, and we talked loudly above the gale.

Crossing, at last, the frozen mill-stream—whose wheel in summer still turned a barren mechanism—we climbed up to Joseph's farm. Sheltered by trees, warm on its bed of snow, it seemed always to be like this. As always it was late; as always this was our final call. The snow had a fine crust upon it, and the old trees sparkled like tinsel.

We grouped ourselves round the farmhouse porch. The sky cleared, and broad streams of stars ran down over the valley and away to Wales. On Slad's white slopes, seen through the black sticks of its woods, some red lamps still burned in the windows.

Everything was quiet; everywhere there was the faint crackling silence of the winter night. We started singing, and we were all moved by the words and the sudden trueness of our voices. Pure, very clear, and breathless we sang:

> As Joseph was a-walking
> He heard an angel sing;
> 'This night shall be the birth-time
> Of Christ the Heavenly King.
>
> He neither shall be bornèd
> In Housen nor in hall,
> Nor in a place of paradise
> But in an ox's stall. . . .'

And 2,000 Christmasses became real to us then; the houses, the halls, the places of paradise had all been visited; the stars were bright to guide the Kings through the snow; and across the farmyard we could hear the beasts in their stalls. We were given roast apples and hot mince-pies, in our nostrils were spices like myrrh, and in our wooden box, as we headed back for the village, there were golden gifts for all.

from *Cider With Rosie*

Those Who at Christmas do Repine
Anonymous

Those who at Christmas do repine,
  And would fain hence dispatch him,
May the with old Duke Humphry dine,
  Or else may Squire Ketch catch 'em.

Remember, O Thou Man
Anonymous

Remember Adam's fall,
  O thou man, O thou man,
Remember Adam's fall
  From Heaven to Hell.
Remember Adam's fall;
How he hath condemned all
In Hell perpetual
  There for to dwell.

Remember God's goodness,
  O thou man, O thou man,
Remember God's goodness

And promise made:
Remember God's goodness,
How His only son he sent,
Our sins for to redress:
    Be not afraid.

The angels all did sing,
    O thou man, O thou man,
The angels all did sing,
    On Sion hill:
The angels all did sing
Praise to our heavenly King,
And peace to man living,
    With right good will.

To Bethlem did they go,
    O thou man, O thou man,
To Bethlem did they go,
    This thing to see:
To Bethlem did they go,
To see if it was so,
If Christ was born or no,
    To set us free.

In Bethlem was He born,
    O thou man, O thou man,
In Bethlem was He born,
    For mankind dear:
In Bethlem was He born
For us that were forlorn,
And therefore took no scorn,
    Our sins to bear.

Give thanks to God alway,
    O thou man, O thou man,

Give thanks to God alway,
With hearts most jolly:
Upon this blessèd day;
Let all men sing and say,
Holy holy.

A Christmas Service
Samuel Pepys

Christmas Day, 1662. Had a pleasant walk to White Hall where I intended to have received the communion with the family, but I come a little too late. So I walked up into the house and spent my time looking over pictures, particularly the ships in King Henry the VIIIth's voyage to Bullaen [Boulogne]; marking the great difference between those built then and now. By and by down to the chapel again, where the Bishop Morley preached upon the song of the Angels, 'Glory to God on high, on earth peace, and good will towards men.' Methought he made but a poor sermon, but long, and reprehending the common jollity of the Court for the true joy that shall and ought to be on these days. Particularized concerning their excess in playes and gaming, saying that he whose office it is to keep the gamesters in order and within bounds, serves but for a second rather in a duell, meaning the groome-porter. Upon which it was worth observing how far they are come from taking the reprehensions of a bishop seriously, that they all laugh in the chapel when he reflected on their ill actions and courses. He did much press us to joy in these publick days of joy, and to hospitality. But one that stood by whispered in my eare that the Bishop do not spend one groate to the poor himself. The sermon done, a good anthem followed with vialls, and the King come down to receive the Sacrament.

For Them
Eleanor Farjeon

Before you bid, for Christmas' sake,
    Your guests to sit at meat,
Oh please to save a little cake
    For them that have no treat.

Before you go down party-dressed
    In silver gown or gold,
Oh please to send a little vest
    To them that still go cold.

Before you give your girl and boy
    Gay gifts to be undone,
Oh please to spare a little toy
    To them that will have none.

Before you gather round the tree
    To dance the day about,
Oh please to give a little glee
    To them that go without.

The Mouse that Didn't Believe in Santa Claus
Eugene Field

The clock stood, of course, in the corner; a moonbeam floated idly on the floor, and a little mauve mouse came from the hole in the chimney corner and frisked and scampered in the light of the moonbeam upon the floor. The little mauve mouse was particularly merry; sometimes she danced upon two legs and sometimes upon four legs, but always very daintily and always very merrily.

'Ah, me,' sighed the old clock, 'how different mice are nowadays from the mice we used to have in the old times! Now there was your grandma, Mistress Velvetpaw, and there was your grandpa, Master Sniffwhisker—how grave and dignified they were! Many a night have I seen them dancing upon the carpet below me, but always that stately minuet and never that crazy frisking which you are executing now, to my surprise— yes, and to my horror, too!'

'But why shouldn't I be merry?' asked the little mauve mouse. 'Tomorrow is Christmas, and this is Christmas Eve.'

'So it is,' said the old clock. 'I had really forgotten all about it. But, tell me, what is Christmas to you, little Miss Mauve Mouse?'

'A great deal to me!' cried the little mauve mouse. 'I have been very good for a very long time; I have not used any bad words, nor have I gnawed any holes, nor have I stolen any canary seed, nor have I worried my mother by running behind the flour barrel where that horrid trap is set. In fact, I have been so good that I'm very sure Santa Claus will bring me something very pretty.'

This seemed to amuse the old clock mightily; in fact, the old clock fell to laughing so heartily that in an unguarded moment she struck twelve instead of ten, which was exceedingly careless.

'Why, you silly little mauve mouse,' said the old clock, 'you don't believe in Santa Claus, do you?'

'Of course I do,' answered the mauve mouse. 'Believe in Santa Claus? Why shouldn't I? Didn't Santa Claus bring me a beautiful butter cracker last Christmas, and a lovely ginger-snap, and a delicious rind of cheese, and—lots of things? I should be very ungrateful if I did *not* believe in Santa Claus, and I certainly shall not disbelieve in him at the very moment when I am expecting him to arrive with a bundle of goodies for me.

'I once had a little sister,' continued the little mauve mouse, 'who did not believe in Santa Claus, and the very thought of the fate that befell her makes my blood run cold and my whiskers stand on end. She died before I was born, but my mother has told me all·about her. Her name was Squeaknibble, and she was in stature one of those long, low, rangey mice that are seldom found in well-stocked pantries. Mother says that Squeaknibble took after our ancestors who came from New England, and seemed to inherit many ancestral traits, the most conspicuous of which was a disposition to sneer at some of the most respected dogmas in mousedom. From her very infancy she doubted, for example, the widely accepted theory that the moon was composed of green cheese; and this heresy was the first intimation her parents had of her sceptical turn of mind. Of course, her parents were vastly annoyed, for they saw that this youthful scepticism would lead to serious, if not fatal, consequences. Yet all in vain did they reason and plead with their headstrong and heretical child.

'For a long time Squeaknibble would not believe that there

was any such arch-fiend as a cat; but she came to be convinced one memorable night, on which occasion she lost two inches of her beautiful tail, and received so terrible a fright that for fully an hour afterward her little heart beat so violently as to lift her off her feet and bump her head against the top of our domestic hole. The cat that deprived my sister of so large a percentage of her tail was the same ogress that nowadays steals into this room, crouches treacherously behind the sofa, and feigns to be asleep, hoping, forsooth, that some of us, heedless of her hated presence, will venture within reach of her claws. So enraged was this ferocious monster at the escape of my sister that she ground her fangs viciously together, and vowed to take no pleasure in life until she held in her devouring jaws the inno-cent little mouse which belonged to the mangled bit of tail she even then clutched in her remorseless claws.'

'Yes,' said the old clock, 'now that you recall the incident, I recollect it well. I was here then, and I remember that I laughed at the cat and chided her for her awkwardness. My reproaches irritated her; she told me that a clock's duty was to run itself down, *not* to be depreciating the merits of others! Yes, I recall the time; that cat's tongue is fully as sharp as her claws.'

'Be that as it may,' said the little mauve mouse, 'it is a matter of history, and therefore beyond dispute, that from that very moment the cat pined for Squeaknibble's life; it seemed as if that one little two-inch taste of Squeaknibble's tail had filled the cat with a consuming appetite for the rest of Squeak-nibble. So the cat waited and watched and hunted and schemed and devised and did everything possible for a cat— a cruel cat—to do in order to gain her murderous ends.

'One night—one fatal Christmas Eve—our mother had undressed the children for bed, and was urging upon them to go to sleep earlier than usual, since she fully expected that Santa Claus would bring each of them something very nice before morning. Thereupon the little dears whisked their cunning tails, pricked up their beautiful ears, and began telling

70

one another what they hoped Santa Claus would bring. One asked for a slice of Roquefort, another for Swiss, another for Brick, and a fourth for Edam; one expressed a preference for cream cheese, while another hoped for Camembert. There were fourteen little ones then, and consequently there were diverse opinions as to the kind of gift which Santa Claus should best bring; still there was, as you can readily understand, an enthusiastic agreement upon this point, namely, that the gift should be cheese of some brand or other.

' "My dears," said our mother, "we should be content with whatsoever Santa Claus bestows, so long as it is cheese, disjoined from all traps whatsoever, unmixed with Paris green, and free from glass, strychnine, and other harmful ingredients. As for myself, I shall be satisfied with a cut of nice, fresh American cheese. So run away to your dreams now, that Santa may find you sleeping."

'The children obeyed—all but Squeaknibble. "Let the others think what they please," said she, "but *I* don't believe in Santa Claus. I'm not going to bed, either. I'm going to creep out of this dark hole and have a quiet romp, all by myself, in the moonlight." Oh, what a vain, foolish, wicked little mouse was Squeaknibble! But I will not reproach the dead; her punishment came all too swiftly. Now listen: who do you suppose overheard her talking so disrespectfully of Santa Claus?'

'Why, Santa Claus himself,' said the old clock.

'Oh, no,' answered the little mauve mouse. 'It was that wicked murderous cat! Just as Satan lurks and lies in wait for bad children, so does the cruel cat lurk and lie in wait for naughty little mice. And you can depend upon it that, when that awful cat heard Squeaknibble speak so disrespectfully of Santa Claus, her wicked eyes glowed with joy, her sharp teeth watered, and her bristling fur emitted electric sparks as big as peas. Then what did that bloody monster do but scuttle as fast as she could into Dear-my-Soul's room, leap up into Dear-my-Soul's crib, and walk off with the pretty little white

71

muff which Dear-my-Soul used to wear when she went for a visit to the little girl in the next block! What upon earth did the horrid old cat want with Dear-my-Soul's pretty little white muff? Ah, the ingenuity of that cat! Listen.

'In the first place,' resumed the little mauve mouse, after a pause that showed the depth of her emotion, 'in the first place, that wretched cat dressed herself up in that pretty little white muff, by which you are to understand that she crawled through the muff just so far as to leave her four cruel legs at liberty.'

'Yes, I understand,' said the old clock.

'Then she put on the boy doll's cap,' said the little mauve mouse, 'and when she was arrayed in the boy doll's fur cap and Dear-my-Soul's pretty little white muff, of course she didn't look like a cruel cat at all. But whom did she look like?'

'Like the boy doll,' suggested the old clock.

'No, no!' cried the little mauve mouse.

'Like Dear-my-Soul? asked the old clock.

'How stupid you are!' exclaimed the little mauve mouse. 'Why, she looked like Santa Claus, of course!'

'Oh, yes; I see,' said the old clock. 'Now I begin to be interested; go on.'

'Alas!' sighed the little mauve mouse, 'not much remains to be told; but there is more of my story left than there was of Squeaknibble when that horrid cat crawled out of that miserable disguise. You are to understand that, contrary to her mother's warning, Squeaknibble issued from the friendly hole in the chimney corner, and gamboled about over this very carpet, and, I dare say, in this very moonlight.

'Right merrily was Squeaknibble gamboling,' continued the little mauve mouse, 'and she had just turned a double somersault without the use of what remained of her tail, when, all of a sudden, she beheld, looming up like a monster ghost, a figure all in white fur! Oh, how frightened she was, and how her little heart did beat! "Purr, purr-r-r," said the ghost in white fur. "Oh, please don't hurt me!" pleaded Squeaknibble. "No;

72

I'll not hurt you," said the ghost in white fur; "I'm Santa Claus, and I've brought you a beautiful piece of savoury old cheese, you dear little mousie, you.' Poor Squeaknibble was deceived; a sceptic all her life, she was at last befooled by the most fatal of frauds. "How good of you!" said Squeaknibble. "I didn't believe there was a Santa Claus, and—" but before she could say more she was seized by two sharp, cruel claws that conveyed her crushed body to the murderous mouth of the cat. I can dwell no longer upon this harrowing scene. Before the morrow's sun rose upon the spot where that tragedy had been enacted, poor Squeaknibble passed to that bourne to which two inches of her beautiful tail had preceded her by the space of three weeks to a day. As for Santa Claus, when he came that Christmas Eve, bringing cheese and goodies for the other little mice, he heard with sorrow of Squeaknibble's fate; and ere he departed he said that in all his experience he had never known of a mouse or a child that had prospered after once saying he didn't believe in Santa Claus.'

Ceremonies for Christmas
Robert Herrick

Come, bring with a noise,
My merry, merry boys,
The Christmas log to the firing;
While my good dame, she
Bids ye all be free;
And drink to your heart's desiring.

With the last year's brand
Light the new block, and
For good success in his spending,
On your psalteries play,
That sweet luck may
Come while the log is a-tending.

Drink now the strong beer,
Cut the white loaf here,
The while the meat is shredding;
For the rare mince-pie
And the plums stand by
To fill the paste that's a-kneading.

Yule! Yule!
Anonymous

Yule! Yule!
Three puddings in a pool;
Crack nuts and cry Yule!

Sir Roger de Coverley at Christmas
Joseph Addison

Sir Roger, after the laudable custom of his ancestors, always keeps open house at Christmas. I learned from him that he had killed eight fat hogs for this season, that he had dealt about his chines very liberally amongst his neighbours, and that in particular he had sent a string of hogs-puddings with a pack of cards to every poor family in the parish. 'I have often thought,' says Sir Roger, 'it happens very well that Christmas should fall out in the middle of winter. It is the most dead, uncomfortable time of the year, when the poor people suffer very much from their poverty and cold, if they had not good cheer, warm fires, and Christmas gambols to support them. I love to rejoice their poor hearts at this season, and to see the whole village merry in my great hall. I allow a double quantity of malt to my small beer and set it a-running for twelve days to everyone that calls for it. I have always a piece of cold beef and a mince-pie upon the table, and am wonderfully pleased to see my tenants pass away a whole evening in playing their innocent tricks.'

Christmas Boxes

Why are the presents of money given at Christmas time known as Christmas Boxes? Because from Roman times onwards it was the custom to make little clay pots with slits in the side just big enough to take a coin. These pots were known as boxes— sometimes 'thrift boxes'—and had to be broken to get the money out. Sometimes they were made in the shape of a pig, because a pig (unlike a sheep or a hen) is of no use to man until it is killed.

New Prince, New Pomp
Robert Southwell

Behold, a silly tender babe
   In freezing winter night
In homely manger trembling lies,
   Alas, a piteous sight!

The inns are full; no man will yield
   This little pilgrim bed,
But forced he is with silly beasts
   In crib to shroud his head.

Despise him not for lying there,
   First, what he is inquire;
An orient pearl is often found
   In depth of dirty mire.

Weigh not his crib, his wooden dish,
   Nor beasts that by him feed;
Weigh not his mother's poor attire,
   Nor Joseph's simple weed.

This stable is a prince's court,
   This crib his chair of state;
The beasts are parcel of his pomp,
   The wooden dish his plate.

The person is that poor attire
  His royal liveries wear;
The Prince Himself is come from heaven;
  This pomp is prizèd there.

With joy approach, O Christian wight,
  Do homage to thy King;
And highly praise His humble pomp,
  Which he from heaven doth bring.

Ballyutility's Christmas Tree
Janet McNeill

Maybe you know the village of Ballyutility. If you've been through it in the train you must have noticed the tidy back gardens, all planted out with orderly potatoes and plump cabbages—there isn't a square inch of ground wasted or a pod of peas that could hold another pea. If you go through the single street you'll find there isn't much in the way of front gardens—most of the houses just have a little square of gravel, except the house at the corner where there is a straggling fir tree. You won't find any children playing in the street either —they've generally got something better to do, and nobody whistles, except to call up a dog. Nobody sings either, except the children in the school, and that's a lesson, so it's different. And when a stranger goes by the dogs take it in turns to bark. That's what it's like in Ballyutility.

Or rather that's what it was like. But something happened last Christmas in Ballyutility, and that's what I want to tell you about. Early in December if you'd gone through the village you'd hardly have known what month it was. You might have heard the children in the school practising carols for the Boxing Day Concert in aid of the Deserving Poor, but there wasn't any sign of Christmas to be seen in any of the three shop windows—the Grocer, the Chemist or the Post Office. Everyone was busy in Ballyutility, but then everybody always was. Mr Jamison, the Grocer, was perhaps the busiest of all—he certainly thought he was. But he didn't festoon his shop with paper chains just because Christmas was coming, nor did he spread it over with artificial frost, or put blobs of cotton wool hanging on strings down the window to look like snow. It wasn't that he didn't know all about these things, for when he was a boy Mr Jamison was apprenticed to his uncle who had a grocer's shop in Belfast, and the week before Christmas his uncle and he had stayed late night after night, sticking blobs of cottonwool on bits of string, till the window was a whirling fairyland, and neither of them grudged the time they spent at it or the clearing up afterwards. But since he had set up shop for himself in Ballyutility Mr Jamison had changed. 'A shop's a shop, not a scene out of a pantomime,' he said. So though the window was full of raisins and sultanas and currants, of candied peel and almonds, of cherries and preserved ginger, of nutmeg and cinnamon and spice and icing sugar, they all sat in their packets in neat and tidy rows, and there wasn't a cottonwool snowflake or a sprig of holly to be seen.

While Mr Jamison was busy making money in his shining shop Mrs Jamison was busy in her shining house, bringing up Anna and Effie and Jane and little Ben. Effie and Jane and little Ben had just got over the whooping cough, and what with wrapping them up in extra warm mufflers every time they went out and unwrapping them again every time they came in, she had been busier than usual. Perhaps that was why she didn't notice how much of her time Anna was spending in the house next door. Mrs McIlvenny and Hughie lived in the house next door—it was the corner house, the one with the fir tree outside it—and Anna and Hughie were the same age, and had always been great friends. But Hughie had spent a year in a hospital in Belfast and was just home and had a couple of months yet to lie in bed.

A couple of days before Christmas Mrs Jamison went into her back garden to hang out her dishcloths and found Mrs McIlvenny doing the same thing in hers. 'How's Hughie keeping today?' asked Mrs Jamison, taking the last of the clothes-pegs out of her mouth.

'He's coming on,' said Mrs McIlvenny, 'but it's not a thing you can hurry. Your Anna is up in the room with him now.'

'Is that where Anna is?' said Mrs Jamison, rather vexed. 'She slipped off when she had the dishes done, and I don't believe she has her lessons half learned. Will you call her down for me?'

'Ah, don't call her down,' Mrs McIlvenny begged, 'Hughie's always extra glad to see Anna. She helps him to put in his time.'

'It seems a sin to have that much time to waste,' Mrs Jamison said, and suddenly wondered what she was thinking of, wasting her own time gossiping over the garden fence. There was plenty to do in the house without this. So she hurried indoors and took out her knitting, and was soon busy on the pair of gloves she was making for little Ben's Christmas present. The pattern book she was using said white fluffy wool with scarlet rabbits embroidered on them, but Mrs Jamison was doing them in grey, which was much more serviceable, and leaving out the rabbits. Even little Ben had enough sense to know that rabbits weren't scarlet! So she sat and knitted, making the needles click and dance up and down the rows, and listened to Effie and Jane murmuring and whooping over their homework, and she wished Anna would come home instead of wasting her time next door with Hughie McIlvenny.

But Anna wasn't wasting her time; she was sitting on the end of Hughie's bed, with her schoolbag on her knee, and the two of them were very busy indeed.

'See what I've brought for you today,' said Anna, taking some great plump fir-cones out of her bag. 'I juked in at the minister's gate on my way home from school. There's hundreds of them just lying about on the grass.'

'Those are grand,' said Hughie, 'but there's only a wee lick of the silver paint left at the bottom of the bottle. What else have you got, Anna?'

She dived into the bag again. 'Here's the tops off the lemonade bottles from the shop. If we hang them in long strings they'll turn in the wind, and the lights will shine on them.'

'They'll be like strings of stars,' Hughie cried. 'What else have you?'

'Silver paper from tangerines, and gold paper off the vinegar bottles,' Anna said, smoothing the shining sheets lovingly, 'but wait till you see here! Easy, Hughie, you'll have them broken.'

'What is it?' Hughie breathed, his eyes alight.

'The electric fused at the Bible Class on Wednesday, and when Mr Simpson was changing the bulbs I got him to give me the duds. You could paint them up with shiny paint, couldn't you, Hughie?'

'They had real lights that lit up on the Christmas tree at the Hospital,' said Hughie, 'green lights and blue lights and red lights. I wish we had real lights.'

'It's no good wishing,' Anna said stoutly, 'but if I fix my bicycle lamp at the bottom of the tree it'll throw its light up through the branches. And there'll be the light from the street lamp, and the light from your room.'

'Did you bring *Her*?' Hughie asked.

'I did. Here she is,' said Anna, tenderly unwrapping the tissue paper from her last package, 'look Hughie!'

Hughie gasped. 'My—oh! Isn't she grand? Why do you never play with her, Anna?'

'Mother says dolls are a waste of time,' Anna answered; 'it was my Auntie from Belfast that bought her for me—the same Auntie that gave me the yellow beads. I never got wearing them either. Mother put them away.'

'She's a beauty,' said Hughie, taking the doll carefully in his hands, 'I'll make her wings and a little wand, and a silver crown for her hair.'

'Oh Hughie,' cried Anna, in sudden distress, 'I've just thought! What'll we do if it rains? Look at her lovely curly hair! She'll be ruined!'

'It'll not rain,' Hughie said, lying back again on his pillows, for he was tired with the excitement, 'it couldn't rain on Christmas Eve.'

Hughie was right, it didn't rain. Christmas Eve was fine and still and starlit. But the shops shut at their usual time in Ballyutility, for everyone had made shopping lists, and had bought their presents long ago. There were no carol singers about either, because the school children were to sing their carols at the Boxing Day Concert (in aid of the Fund for the Deserving Poor) so there wasn't any need for them to sing them twice, was there? Ballyutility village street was deserted, everyone was indoors having their tea or tying up their presents with brown paper and string—brown paper that would come in useful for parcels afterwards—so no one saw Anna Jamison when she came cautiously out of her back-door, carrying her mother's step-ladder.

Half an hour later the schoolmistress, who had not lived long enough in Ballyutility to be as clever at arranging her Christmas as everyone else, stepped out into the street to post a Christmas card to an aunt whom she had forgotten about. But no sooner had she stepped out than she stepped back again, and called to Tommy, her landlady's little boy, who was cleaning the shoes in the scullery to 'come and look'.

'I declare to goodness,' said Tommy wonderingly, as he stood in the doorway with the blacking brushes still in his hands, 'I declare to goodness—it's—a Christmas Tree.'

'Come on in out of that, Tommy,' his mother called, 'what

are you standing there for? There's a whole pile of shoes waiting on you.'

'This is one night they may wait,' declared Tommy, and banging down the brushes he was away out into the street, hatless and coatless, knocking on Mrs Jamison's door.

'Come on,' he cried, hammering on the door with his fists, 'come on till you see! Effie! Jane! Come on out, the whole lot of you. The tree! The tree!'

'Come back!' called Mrs Jamison, as Effie and Jane ran out to look, leaving the door wide open behind them, 'come back at once. Effie! Jane! You'll catch your death.'

But it was no use telling them to come back. For they were away—to stand—and gaze—and run and knock on other doors, and bring more wondering children to see the fir tree, transformed in all its fantastic finery, jewelled and adorned, and magically lit by the bicycle lamp, the street lamp, and the light that poured down from Hughie's bedroom. And Hughie from his window was looking down on a flower-bed of children's faces, upturned to the tree, fringed by a crowd of anxious mothers who had followed them out with coats and scarves.

'All those strings of shining stars,' declared one child, as the wind set the lemonade tops swinging and turning, 'as many stars as there are in the sky.'

'What a lot of time it must have taken,' said his mother who was standing behind him, 'and what a waste of time too!'

'What a waste!' echoed the children dutifully.

'Silver fir cones,' cried a little girl, 'just as if they were all covered with frost. Look how beautifully they sparkle!'

'What a waste of paint!' declared her mother, and the children breathed again in chorus. 'What a waste! What a waste!'

'Would you look at the fairy at the top!' piped up the smallest girl of all, 'golden wings she has! And a crown! And look at her lovely hair!'

'If it rains,' said her mother, 'her hair will be ruined. What a waste! It will all be wasted!'

'What a waste!' cried the children all together, 'what a lovely waste! What a lovely, *lovely* waste!'

Then they were all very quiet. Someone in the back row called out, 'Here's Mr Jamison coming!' and everbody stood back a little to let Mr Jamison through.

'A crowd in the streets at this time of night!' he declared. 'These children ought to be in their beds. What's it all about? What sort of a carry-on's this? A tree! A Christmas tree!'

'Isn't it lovely, Mr Jamison?' said the smallest girl of all, without taking her eyes off the tree, 'Look at those stars—and the fairy at the top.'

Mr Jamison stood and looked. Then he said slowly, 'It needs the snow. That's what it needs—the snow.'

One boy at the back, who was bolder than the others, piped up:

> Good King Wenceslas looked out
>   On the Feast of Stephen,
> When the snow lay round about
>   Deep and crisp and even.

And before he had finished the verse they were all singing with him.

So Ballyutility had its Christmas Eve—and its Christmas, too. Little Ben Jamison, who had slept through all the excitement, was taken out by his big sister Anna on Christmas morning. Anna was wearing her yellow beads, and first he pulled at these, but when he saw the tree he crowed and chuckled and clapped his hands which were fine and warm in the new gloves his mother had given him (with scarlet rabbits on the backs— his mother had sat up very late when she went in from the Christmas tree the night before). Although there were now no lights on the tree it looked just as lovely, for it was covered with cascades of cottonwool snow from head to foot. (Mr Jamison had knocked up the chemist and bought all the cottonwool in the shop, and he had gone to bed very late too.)

If you try to visit Ballyutility now you won't be able to find it because they've changed the name of the place. The new name was in the paper the other day; they'd won a prize for the best display of flowers in the village street. The new name is much nicer than the old one was. They chose it just because they liked the sound of it. It's a beautiful name, but it doesn't mean a thing.

from A Pinch of Salt

To His Saviour, A Child, A Present By A Child
Robert Herrick

Go pretty child, and bear this flower
Unto thy little Saviour;
And tell Him, by that bud now blown,
He is the Rose of Sharon known;
When thou hast said so, stick it there
Upon His bib, or stomacher:
And tell Him (for good handsel too)
That thou hast brought a whistle new,
Made of clean straight oaken reed,
To charm His cries (at time of need;)
Tell Him, for choral, thou hast none;
But if thou hadst, He should have one;
But poor thou art, and knows to be
Even as moneyless as He.

Lastly, if thou canst win a kiss
From those mellifluous lips of His;
Then never take a second on,
To spoil the first impression.

I Saw Three Ships
Traditional

I saw three ships come sailing by,
  On Christmas Day, on Christmas Day,
I saw three ships come sailing by,
  On Christmas Day in the morning.

And who was in those ships all three,
  On Christmas Day, on Christmas Day,
And who was in those ships all three,
  On Christmas Day in the morning?

Our Saviour Christ and His Lady,
  On Christmas Day, on Christmas Day,
Our Saviour Christ and His Lady,
  On Christmas Day in the morning

Oh! they sailed into Bethlehem,
  On Christmas Day, on Christmas Day,
Oh! they sailed into Bethlehem,
  On Christmas Day in the morning.

And all the bells on earth shall ring,
On Christmas Day, on Christmas Day,
And all the bells on earth shall ring,
On Christmas Day in the morning.

And all the Angels in Heaven shall sing,
On Christmas Day, on Christmas Day,
And all the Angels in Heaven shall sing,
On Christmas Day in the morning.

And all the souls on earth shall sing,
On Christmas Day, on Christmas Day,
And all the souls on earth shall sing,
On Christmas Day in the morning.

Christmas is Coming
Alison Uttley

At Christmas the wind ceased to moan. Snow lay thick on the fields and the woods cast blue shadows across it. The fir trees were like sparkling, gem-laden Christmas trees, the only ones Susan had ever seen. The orchard, with the lacy old boughs outlined with snow, was a grove of fairy trees. The woods were enchanted, exquisite, the trees were holy, and anything harmful had shrunken to a thin wisp and had retreated into the depths.

The fields lay with their unevennesses gone and paths obliterated, smooth white slopes criss-crossed by black lines running up to the woods. More than ever the farm seemed under a spell, like a toy in the forest, with little wooden animals and men; a brown horse led by a stiff little red-scarfed man to a yellow stable door; round, white, woolly sheep clustering round a blue trough of orange mangolds; red cows drinking from a square, white trough, and returning to a painted cow-house.

Footprints were everywhere on the snow, rabbits and foxes, blackbirds, pheasants and partridges, trails of small paws, the mark of a brush, and the long feet of the cock pheasant and the tip-mark of his tail.

A jay flew out of the wood like a blue flashing diamond and came to the grass-plot for bread. A robin entered the house and hopped under the table while Susan sat very still and her father sprinkled crumbs on the floor.

Rats crouched outside the window, peeping out of the walls with gleaming eyes, seizing the birds' crumbs and scraps, and slowly lolloping back again.

Red squirrels ran along the walls to the back door, close to the window, to eat the crumbs on the bench where the milk cans froze. Every wild animal felt that a truce had come with the snow, and they visited the house where there was food in plenty, and sat with paws uplifted and noses twitching.

For the granaries were full, it had been a prosperous year, and there was food for everyone. Not like the year before when there was so little hay that Mr Garland had to buy a stack in February. Three large haystacks as big as houses stood in the stackyard, thatched evenly and straight by Job Fletcher, who was the best thatcher for many a mile. Great mounds showed where the roots were buried. The brick-lined pit was filled with grains and in the barns were stores of corn.

The old brew-house was full of logs of wood, piled high against the walls, cut from trees which the wind had blown down. The coal-house with its strong ivied walls, part of the old fortress, had been stored with coal brought many a mile in the blaze of summer; twenty tons lay under the snow.

On the kitchen walls hung the sides of bacon and from hooks

in the ceiling dangled great hams and shoulders. Bunches of onions were twisted in the pantry and barn, and an empty cow-house was stored with potatoes for immediate use.

The floor of the apple chamber was covered with apples, rosy apples, little yellow ones, like cowslip balls, wizenedy apples with withered, wrinkled cheeks, fat, well-fed smooth-faced apples, and immense green cookers, pointed like a house, which would burst in the oven and pour out a thick cream of the very essence of apples.

Even the cheese chamber had its cheeses this year, for there had been too much milk for the milkman, and the cheese presses had been put into use again. Some of them were Christmas cheese, with layers of sage running through the middles like green ribbons.

Stone jars like those in which the forty thieves hid stood on the pantry floor, filled with white lard, and balls of fat tied up in bladders hung from the hooks. Along the broad shelves round the walls were pots of jam, blackberry and apple, from the woods and orchard, Victoria plum from the trees on house and barn, black currant from the garden, and red currant jelly, damson cheese from the half-wild ancient trees which grew everywhere, leaning over walls, dropping their blue fruit on paths and walls, in pigsty and orchard, in field and water trough, so that Susan thought they were wild as hips and haws.

Pickles and spices filled old brown pots decorated with crosses and flowers, like the pitchers and crocks of Will Shakespeare's time.

In the little dark wine chamber under the stairs were bottles of elderberry wine, purple, thick, and sweet, and golden cowslip wine, and hot ginger, some of them many years old, waiting for the winter festivities.

There were dishes piled with mince pies on the shelves of the larder, and a row of plum puddings with their white calico caps, and strings of sausages, and round pats of butter, with swans and cows and wheat-ears printed upon them.

Everyone who called at the farm had to eat and drink at Christmas-tide.

A few days before Christmas Mr Garland and Dan took a bill-hook and knife and went into the woods to cut branches of scarlet-berried holly. They tied them together with ropes and dragged them down over the fields to the barn. Mr Garland cut a bough of mistletoe from the ancient hollow hawthorn which leaned over the wall by the orchard, and thick clumps of dark-berried ivy from the walls.

Indoors, Mrs Garland and Susan and Becky polished and rubbed and cleaned the furniture and brasses, so that everything glowed and glittered. They decorated every room, from the kitchen where every lustre jug had its sprig in its mouth, every brass candlestick had its chaplet, every copper saucepan and preserving-pan had its wreath of shining berries and leaves, through the hall, which was a bower of green, to the two parlours which were festooned and hung with holly and boughs of fir, and ivy berries dipped in red raddle, left over from sheep marking.

Holly decked every picture and ornament. Sprays hung over the bacon and twisted round the hams and herb bunches. The clock carried a crown on his head, and every dish-cover had a little sprig. Susan kept an eye on the lonely forgotten humble things, the jelly moulds and colanders and nutmeg-graters, and made them happy with glossy leaves. Everything seemed to speak, to ask for its morsel of greenery, and she tried to leave out nothing.

On Christmas Eve fires blazed in the kitchen and parlour and even in the bedrooms. Becky ran from room to room with the red-hot salamander which she stuck between the bars to make a blaze, and Mrs Garland took the copper warming-pan filled with glowing cinders from the kitchen fire and rubbed it between the sheets of all the beds. Susan had come down to her cosy tiny room with thick curtains at the window, and a fire in the big fireplace. Flames roared up the chimneys as Dan carried in the logs and Becky piled them on the blaze. The wind came back and tried to get in, howling at the key-holes, but all the shutters were cottered and the doors shut. The horses and mares stood in the stables, warm and happy, with nodding heads. The cows slept in the cow-houses, the sheep in the open sheds. Only Rover stood at the door of his kennel, staring up at the sky, howling to the dog in the moon, and then he, too, turned and lay down in his straw.

In the middle of the kitchen ceiling there hung the kissing-bunch, the best and brightest pieces of holly made in the shape of a large ball which dangled from the hook. Silver and gilt drops, crimson bells, blue glass trumpets, bright oranges and red polished apples, peeped and glittered through the glossy leaves. Little flags of all nations, but chiefly Turkish for some unknown reason, stuck out like quills on a hedgehog. The lamp hung near, and every little berry, every leaf, every pretty ball and apple had a tiny yellow flame reflected in its heart.

Twisted candles hung down, yellow, red, and blue, unlighted but gay, and on either side was a string of paper lanterns.

Mrs Garland climbed on a stool and nailed on the wall the Christmas texts, 'God bless our Home', 'God is Love', 'Peace be on this House', 'A Happy Christmas and a Bright New Year'.

So the preparations were made. Susan hung up her stocking at the foot of the bed and fell asleep. But soon singing roused her and she sat, bewildered. Yes, it was the carol-singers.

Outside under the stars she could see the group of men and women, with lanterns throwing beams across the paths and on to the stable door. One man stood apart beating time, another played a fiddle and another had a flute. The rest sang in four parts the Christmas hymns, 'While shepherds watched', 'O come, all ye faithful', and 'Hark the herald angels sing'.

There was the Star, Susan could see it twinkling and bright in the dark boughs with their white frosted layers; and there was the stable. In a few hours it would be Christmas Day, the best day of all the year.

from *The Country Child*

A Child This Day is Born
Traditional

A child this day is born,
A child of high renown,
Most worthy of a sceptre,
A sceptre and a crown:

   Nowell, Nowell, Nowell,
   Nowell, sing all we may,
   Because the King of all kings
   Was born this blessèd day.

These tidings shepherds heard,
In field watching their fold,
Were by an angel unto them
That night revealed and told:

To whom the angel spoke,
Saying, 'Be not afraid;
Be glad, poor silly[1] shepherds—
Why are you so dismayed?

'For lo! I bring you tidings
Of gladness and of mirth,
Which cometh to all people by
This holy infant's birth':

[1] Simple.

Then there was with the angel
A host incontinent[2]
Of heavenly bright soldiers,
Which from the Highest was sent:

Lauding the Lord our God,
And His celestial King;
All glory be in Paradise,
This heavenly host did sing:

And as the angels told them,
So to them did appear;
They found the young child, Jesus Christ,
With Mary, His mother dear.

Keeping Christmas
Eleanor Farjeon

How will you your Christmas keep?
Feasting, fasting, or asleep?
Will you laugh or will you pray,
Or will you forget the day?

Be it kept with joy or pray'r,
Keep of either some to spare;
Whatsoever brings the day,
Do not keep but give away.

[2] Innumerable.

At Christmas be Merry
Thomas Tusser

At Christmas be merry, and thankful withal,
And feast thy poor neighbours, the great with the small.

Christmas Presents
Susan Coolidge

'What are the children all doing today?' said Katy, laying down *Norway and the Norwegians*, which she was reading for the fourth time: 'I haven't seen them since breakfast.'

Aunt Izzie, who was sewing on the other side of the room, looked up from her work.

'I don't know,' she said, 'they're over at Cecy's, or somewhere. They'll be back before long, I guess.'

Her voice sounded a little odd and mysterious, but Katy didn't notice it.

'I thought of such a nice plan yesterday,' she went on. 'That was that all of them should hang their stockings up here tomorrow night instead of in the nursery. Then I could see them open their presents, you know. Mayn't they, Aunt Izzie! It would be real fun.'

'I don't believe there will be any objection,' replied her aunt. She looked as if she were trying not to laugh. Katy wondered what *was* the matter with her.

It was more than two months now since Cousin Helen went away, and winter had fairly come. Snow was falling outdoors. Katy could see the thick flakes go whirling past the window, but the sight did not chill her. It only made the room look warmer and more cosy. It was a pleasant room now. There was a bright fire in the grate. Everything was neat and orderly, the air was sweet with mignonette, from a little glass of flowers which stood on the table, and the Katy who lay in bed was a very different-looking Katy from the forlorn girl of a few weeks ago.

Cousin Helen's visit, though it lasted only one day, did great good. Not that Katy grew perfect all at once. None of us do that, even in books. But it is everything to be started in the right path. Katy's feet were on it now; and though she often stumbled and slipped, and often sat down discouraged, she kept on pretty steadily, in spite of bad days, which made her say to herself that she was not getting forward at all.

These bad days, when everything seemed hard, and she herself was cross and fretful, and drove the children out of her room, cost Katy many bitter tears. But after them she would pick herself up, and try again, and harder. And I think that in spite of drawbacks, the little scholar, on the whole, was learning her lesson pretty well.

Cousin Helen was a great comfort all this time. She never forgot Katy. Nearly every week some little thing came from her. Sometimes it was a pencil note, written from her sofa. Sometimes it was an interesting book, or a new magazine, or some pretty little thing for the room. The crimson wrapper which Katy wore was one of her presents, so were the bright chromos of autumn leaves which hung on the wall, the little stand for the books—all sorts of things. Katy loved to look about her as she lay. All the room seemed full of Cousin Helen and her kindness.

'I wish I had something pretty to put into everbody's stocking,' she went on, wistfully; 'but I've only got the muffetees for papa, and these reins for Phil.' She took them from under her pillow as she spoke—gay worsted affairs, with bells sewed on here and there. She had knitted them herself, a very little bit at a time.

'There's my pink sash,' she said suddenly; 'I might give that to Clover. I only wore it once, you know, and I don't *think* I got any spots on it. Would you please fetch it and let me see, Aunt Izzie? It's in the top drawer.'

Aunt Izzie brought the sash. It proved to be quite fresh, and they both decided that it would do nicely for Clover.

'You know I shan't want sashes for ever so long,' said Katy, in rather a sad tone. 'And this is a beauty.'

When she spoke next her voice was bright again.

'I wish I had something real nice for Elsie. Do you know, Aunt Izzie—I think Elsie is the dearest little girl that ever was.'

'I'm glad you've found it out,' said Aunt Izzie, who had always been specially fond of Elsie.

'What she wants most of all is a writing-desk,' continued Katy. 'And Johnny wants a sled. But oh, dear! those are such big things. And I've only got two dollars and a quarter.'

Aunt Izzie marched out of the room without saying anything. When she came back she had something folded up in her hand.

'I didn't know what to give you for Christmas, Katy,' she said, 'because Helen sends you such a lot of things that there don't seem to be anything you haven't already. So I thought I'd give you this, and let you choose for yourself. But if you've set your heart on getting presents for the children, perhaps you'd rather have it now.' So saying, Aunt Izzie laid on the bed a crisp, new five-dollar bill.

'How good you are!' cried Katy, flushed with pleasure.

And indeed Aunt Izzie *did* seem to have grown wonderfully good of late. Perhaps Katy had got hold of her smooth handle!

Being now in possession of seven dollars and a quarter, Katy could afford to be gorgeously generous. She gave Aunt Izzie an exact description of the desk she wanted.

'It's no matter about its being very big,' said Katy, 'but it must have a blue velvet lining, and an inkstand with a silver top. And please buy some little sheets of paper and envelopes, and a pen-handle; the prettiest you can find. Oh! and there must be a lock and key. Don't forget that, Aunt Izzie.'

'No, I won't. What else?'

'I'd like the sled to be green,' went on Katy, 'and to have a nice name. "Sky-Scraper" would be nice, if there was one. Johnny saw a sled once called "Sky-Scraper", and she said it was splendid. And if there's money enough left, aunty, won't you buy me a real nice book for Dorry, and another for Cecy, and a silver thimble for Mary? Her old one is full of holes. Oh! and some candy. And something for Debby and Bridget— some little thing, you know. I think that's all!'

Was ever seven dollars and a quarter expected to do so much? Aunt Izzie must have been a witch, indeed, to make it hold out. But she did, and next day all the precious bundles came home. How Katy enjoyed untying the strings!

Everything was exactly right.

'There wasn't any "Sky-Scraper",' said Aunt Izzie, 'so I got "Snow-Skimmer" instead.'

'It's beautiful, and I like it just as well,' said Katy, contentedly.

'Oh, hide them, hide them!' she cried, with sudden terror, 'somebody's coming.' But the somebody was only Papa, who put his head into the room as Aunt Izzie, laden with bundles, scuttled across the hall.

Katy was glad to catch him alone. She had a little private secret to talk over with him. It was about Aunt Izzie, for whom she, as yet, had no present.

'I thought perhaps you'd get me a book like that one of Cousin Helen's, which Aunt Izzie liked so much,' she said. 'I don't recollect the name exactly. It was something about a Shadow. But I've spent all my money.'

'Never mind about that,' said Dr Carr. 'We'll make that right. *The Shadow of the Cross*—was that it? I'll buy it this afternoon.'

'Oh, thank you, Papa! And please get a brown cover, if you can, because Cousin Helen's was brown. And you won't let Aunt Izzie know, will you? Be careful, Papa!'

'I'll swallow the book first, brown cover and all,' said Papa, making a funny face. He was pleased to see Katy so interested about anything again.

These delightful secrets took up so much of her thoughts, that Katy scarcely found time to wonder at the absence of the children, who generally haunted her room, but who for three days back had hardly been seen. However, after supper they all came up in a body, looking very merry, as if they had been having a good time somewhere.

'You don't know what we've been doing,' began Philly.

'Hush, Phil!' said Clover, in a warning voice. Then she divided the stockings which she held in her hand. And everybody proceeded to hang them up.

Dorry hung his on one side of the fireplace, and John hers exactly opposite. Clover and Phil suspended theirs side by side, on two handles of the bureau.

'I'm going to put mine here, close to Katy, so that she can see it the first fing in the morning,' said Elsie, pinning hers to the bed-post.

Then they all sat down round the fire to write their wishes on bits of paper, and see whether they would burn, or fly up the chimney. If they did the latter, it was a sign that Santa Claus had them safe, and would bring the things wished for.

John wished for a sled and a doll's tea-set, and the continuation of the *Swiss Family Robinson*. Dorry's list ran thus:

A plum-cake.

A new Bibel.

Harry and Lucy.

A Kellidescope.

Everything else Santa Claus likes.

When they had written these lists they threw them into the fire. The fire gave a flicker just then, and the papers vanished. Nobody saw exactly how. John thought they flew up the chimney, but Dorry said they didn't.

Phil dropped his piece in very solemnly. It flamed for a minute, then sank into ashes.

'There, you won't get it, whatever it was!' said Dorry. 'What did you write, Phil?'

'Nofing,' said Phil, 'only just Philly Carr.'

The children shouted.

'I wrote a "writing-desk" on mine,' remarked Elsie, sorrowfully, 'but it all burned up.'

Katy chuckled when she heard this.

And now Clover produced her list. She read aloud:

Strive and Thrive.

A pair of kid gloves.

A muff.

A good temper!

Then she dropped it into the fire. Behold, it flew straight up the chimney.

'How queer!' said Katy, 'none of the rest of them did that.'

The truth was, that Clover, who was a canny little mortal, had slipped across the room and opened the door just before putting her wishes in. This, of course, made a draught, and sent the paper right upward.

Pretty soon Aunt Izzie came in and swept them all off to bed.

'I know how it will be in the morning,' she said, 'you'll all be up and racing about as soon as it is light. So you must get your sleep now, if ever.'

After they had gone Katy recollected that nobody had offered to hang a stocking up for her. She felt a little hurt when she thought of it. 'But I suppose they forgot,' she said to herself.

A little later Papa and Aunt Izzie came in, and they filled the stockings. It was great fun. Each was brought to Katy, as she lay in bed, that she might arrange it as she liked.

The toes were stuffed with candy and oranges. Then came the parcels, all shapes and sizes, tied in white paper, with ribbons, and labelled.

'What's that?' asked Dr Carr, as Aunt Izzie rammed a long, narrow package into Clover's stocking.

'A nail-brush,' answered Aunt Izzie; 'Clover needed a new one.'

How Papa and Katy laughed! 'I don't believe Santa Claus ever had such a thing before,' said Dr Carr.

'He's a very dirty old gentleman, then,' observed Aunt Izzie, grimly.

The desk and sled were too big to go into any stocking, so they were wrapped in paper and hung beneath the other things. It was ten o'clock before all was done, and Papa and Aunt Izzie went away. Katy lay a long time watching the queer shapes of the stocking-legs as they dangled in the fire-light. Then she fell asleep.

It seemed only a minute before something touched her and woke her up. Behold, it was daytime, and there was Philly in his night-gown, climbing up on the bed to kiss her! The rest of the children, half dressed, were dancing about with their stockings in their hands.

'Merry Christmas! Merry Christmas!' they cried. 'Oh, Katy, such beautiful, *beautiful* things!'

'Oh!' shrieked Elsie, who at that moment spied the desk, 'Santa Claus *did* bring it, after all! Why, it's got "From Katy" written on it! Oh Katy, it's so sweet, and I'm *so* happy!' and Elsie hugged Katy, and sobbed for pleasure.

But what was that strange thing beside the bed? Katy stared, and rubbed her eyes. It certainly had not been there when she went to sleep. How had it come?

It was a little evergreen tree planted in a red flower-pot. The pot had stripes of gilt paper stuck on it, and gilt stars and crosses, which made it look very gay. The boughs of the tree were hung with oranges, and nuts, and shiny red apples, and pop-corn balls, and strings of bright berries. There were also a number of little packages tied with blue and crimson ribbon, and altogether the tree looked so pretty, that Katy gave a cry of delighted surprise.

'It's a Christmas tree for you, because you're ill, you know!' said the children, all trying to hug her at once.

'We made it ourselves,' said Dorry, hopping about on one foot. 'I pasted the black stars on the pot.'

'And I popped the corn!' cried Philly.

'Do you like it?' asked Elsie, cuddling close to Katy. 'That's my present—that one tied with a green ribbon. I wish it was nicer! Don't you want to open 'em right away?'

Of course Katy wanted to. All sorts of things came out of the little bundles. The children had arranged every parcel themselves. No grown person had been allowed to help in the least.

Elsie's present was a pen-wiper, with a grey flannel kitten on it; Johnnie's, a doll's tea-tray of scarlet tin.

'Isn't it beau-ti-ful?' she said, admiringly.

Dorry's gift, I regret to say, was a huge red-and-yellow spider, which whirled wildly when waved at the end of its string.

'They didn't want me to buy it,' said he, 'but I did! I thought it would amoose you. Does it amoose you, Katy?'

'Yes, indeed,' said Katy, laughing and blinking as Dorry waved the spider to and fro before her eyes.

'You can play with it when we ain't here, and you're all alone, you know,' remarked Dorry, highly gratified.

'But you don't notice what the tree's standing upon,' said Clover.

It was a chair, a very large and curious one, with a long-cushioned back, which ended in a footstool.

'That's Papa's present,' said Clover. 'See, it tips back so as to be just like a bed. And Papa says he thinks pretty soon you can lie on it, in the window, where you can see us play.'

'Does he really?' said Katy, doubtfully. It still hurt her very much to be touched or moved.

'And see what's tied to the arm of the chair,' said Elsie.

It was a little silver bell, with 'Katy' engraved on the handle.

'Cousin Helen sent it. It's for you to ring when you want anybody to come,' explained Elsie.

More surprises. To the other arm of the chair was fastened a beautiful book. It was *The Wide Wide World*—and there was Katy's name written on it, 'From her affectionate Cecy.' On it stood a great parcel of dried cherries from Mrs Hall. Mrs Hall had the most *delicious* dried cherries, the children thought. 'How perfectly lovely everybody is!' said Katy, with grateful tears in her eyes.

That was a pleasant Christmas. The children declared it to be the nicest they had ever had. And though Katy couldn't quite say that, she enjoyed it too, and was very happy.

It was several weeks before she was able to use the chair, but when once she became accustomed to it, it proved very comfortable. Aunt Izzie would dress her in the morning, tip the chair back till it was on a level with the bed, and then, very gently and gradually, draw her over on to it. Wheeling across the room was always painful, but sitting in the window and looking out at the clouds, the people going by, and the children playing in the snow, was delightful. How delightful nobody knows, excepting those who, like Katy, have lain for six months in bed, without a peep at the outside world. Every day she grew brighter and more cheerful.

from *What Katy Did*

A New Year Carol
Traditional

Here we bring new water
    From the well so clear,
For to worship God with
    This happy new year.

Sing levy dew, sing levy dew,
    The water and the wine;
The seven bright gold wires
    And the bugles that do shine.

Sing reign to Fair Maid,
    With gold upon her toe—
Open you the West Door,
    And turn the Old Year go.

Sing reign of Fair Maid,
    With gold upon her chin—
Open you the East Door,
    And let the New Year in.

Sing levy dew, sing levy dew,
    The water and the wine;
The seven bright gold wires
    And the bugles that do shine.

When Icicles Hang by the Wall
William Shakespeare

When icicles hang by the wall,
   And Dick the shepherd blows his nail;
When Tom bears logs into the hall,
   And milk comes frozen home in pail;
When blood is nipped, and ways be foul,
—Then nightly sings the staring owl:
   To-who,
To-whit, To-who—a merry note,
While greasy Joan doth keel[1] the pot.

When all aloud the wind doth blow,
   And coughing drowns the parson's saw,
And birds sit brooding in the snow,
   And Marian's nose looks red and raw;
When roasted crabs[2] hiss in the bowl,
—Then nightly sings the staring owl:
   To-who,
To-whit, To-who—a merry note,
While greasy Joan doth keel the pot.

               from *Love's Labours Lost*

[1] Keep from boiling over.   [2] Crab-apples.

Cries of London
Traditional

Young Patty Smart
  Selling her pastry, cries
'Buy a nice tart!'

Old Mistress Wake
  Morn and afternoon cries
'Hot loaf, hot cake!'

Waiting
James Reeves

Waiting, waiting, waiting
  For the party to begin;
Waiting, waiting, waiting
  For the laughter and the din;
Waiting, waiting, waiting
  With hair just so
And clothes trim and tidy
  From top-knot to toe.

The floor is all shiny,
    The lights are ablaze;
There are sweatmeats in plenty
    And cakes beyond praise.
Oh the games and dancing,
    The tricks and the toys,
The music and the madness
    The colour and noise!
Waiting, waiting, waiting
For the first knock on the door—
Was ever such waiting,
    Such waiting before?

Christmas Pie
George Wither

Lo! now is come our joyfull'st feast!
    Let every man be jolly;
Each room with ivy leaves is dressed,
    And every post with holly.
Now all our neighbours' chimneys smoke,
    And Christmas blocks are burning;
Their ovens they with bakemeats choke,
    And all their spits are turning.
Without the door let sorrow lie,
    And if for cold it hap to die,
We'll bury it in a Christmas pie,
    And ever more be merry.

Bob Cratchit's Christmas
Charles Dickens

Then up rose Mrs Cratchit, Cratchit's wife, dressed out but poorly in a twice-turned gown, but brave in ribbons, which are cheap and make a goodly show for sixpence; and she laid the cloth, assisted by Belinda Cratchit, second of her daughters, also brave in ribbons; while Master Peter Cratchit plunged a fork into the saucepan of potatoes, and getting the corners of his monstrous shirt collar (Bob's private property, conferred upon his son and heir in honour of the day) into his mouth, rejoiced to find himself so gallantly attired, and yearned to show his linen in the fashionable Parks. And now two smaller Cratchits, boy and girl, came tearing in, screaming that outside the baker's they had smelt the goose, and known it for their own; and basking in luxurious thoughts of sage and onion, these young Cratchits danced about the table, and exalted Master Peter Cratchit to the skies, while he (not proud, although his collars nearly choked him) blew the fire, until the slow potatoes bubbling up, knocked loudly at the saucepan lid to be let out and peeled.

'What has ever got your precious father then?' said Mrs Cratchit. 'And your brother, Tiny Tim! And Martha warn't as late last Christmas Day by half-an-hour!'

'Here's Martha, Mother!' said a girl, appearing as she spoke.

'Here's Martha, Mother!' cried the two young Cratchits. 'Hurrah! There's *such* a goose, Martha!'

'Why, bless your heart alive, my dear, how late you are!'

said Mrs Cratchit, kissing her a dozen times, and taking off her shawl and bonnet for her with officious zeal.

'We'd a deal of work to finish up last night,' replied the girl, 'and had to clear away this morning, Mother!'

'Well! Never mind so long as you are come,' said Mrs Cratchit. 'Sit ye down before the fire, my dear, and have a warm, Lord bless ye!'

'No, no! There's Father coming!' cried the two young Cratchits, who were everywhere at once. 'Hide, Martha, hide!'

So Martha hid herself, and in came little Bob, the father, with at least three feet of comforter exclusive of the fringe, hanging down before him; and his threadbare clothes darned up and brushed, to look seasonable; and Tiny Tim upon his shoulder. Alas for Tiny Tim, he bore a little crutch, and had his limbs supported by an iron frame!

'Why, where's our Martha?' cried Bob Cratchit, looking round.

'Not coming,' said Mrs Cratchit.

'Not coming!' said Bob, with a sudden declension in his high spirits; for he had been Tim's blood horse all the way from church, and had come home rampant. 'Not coming upon Christmas Day!'

Martha didn't like to see him disappointed, if it were only in joke; so she came out prematurely from behind the closet door, and ran into his arms, while the two young Cratchits hustled Tiny Tim, and bore him off into the wash-house, that he might hear the pudding singing in the copper.

'And how did little Tim behave?' asked Mrs Cratchit, when she had rallied Bob on his credulity, and Bob had hugged his daughter to his heart's content.

'As good as gold,' said Bob, 'and better. Somehow he gets thoughtful, sitting by himself so much, and thinks the strangest things you ever heard. He told me, coming home, that he hoped the people saw him in the church, because he was a cripple, and it might be pleasant to them to remember upon

Christmas Day, who made lame beggars walk and blind men see.'

Bob's voice was tremulous when he told them this, and trembled more when he said that Tiny Tim was growing strong and hearty.

His active little crutch was heard upon the floor, and back came Tiny Tim before another word was spoken, escorted by his brother and sister to his stool before the fire; and while Bob, turning up his cuffs—as if, poor fellow, they were capable of being made more shabby—compounded some hot mixture in a jug with gin and lemons, and stirred it round and round and put it on the hob to simmer, Master Peter and the two ubiquitous young Cratchits went to fetch the goose, with which they soon returned in high procession.

Such a bustle ensued that you might have thought a goose the rarest of all birds; a feathered phenomenon, to which a black swan was a matter of course, and in truth it was something very like it in that house. Mrs Cratchit made the gravy (ready beforehand in a little saucepan) hissing hot; Master Peter mashed the potatoes with incredible vigour; Miss Belinda sweetened up the apple sauce; Martha dusted the hot plates; Bob took Tiny Tim beside him in a tiny corner at the table; the two young Cratchits set chairs for everybody, not forgetting themselves, and mounting guard upon their posts, crammed spoons into their mouths, lest they should shriek for goose before their turn came to be helped. At last the dishes were set on, and grace was said. It was succeeded by a breathless pause, as Mrs Cratchit, looking slowly all along the carving-knife, prepared to plunge it in the breast; but when she did, and when the long-expected gush of stuffing issued forth, one murmur of delight arose all round the board, and even Tiny Tim, excited by the two young Cratchits, beat on the table with the handle of his knife, and feebly cried Hurrah!

There never was such a goose. Bob said he didn't believe there ever was such a goose cooked. It tenderness and flavour,

size and cheapness, were the themes of universal admiration. Eked out by the apple sauce and mashed potatoes, it was a sufficient dinner for the whole family; indeed, as Mrs Cratchit said with great delight (surveying one small atom of a bone upon the dish), they hadn't ate it all at last! Yet everyone had had enough, and the youngest Cratchits, in particular, were steeped in sage and onion to the eyebrows! But now, the plates being changed by Miss Belinda, Mrs Cratchit left the room alone—too nervous to bear witnesses—to take the pudding up and bring it in.

Suppose it should not be done enough! Suppose it should break in turning out! Suppose somebody should have got over the wall of the back-yard, and stolen it, while they were merry with the goose—a supposition at which the two young Cratchits became livid! All sorts of horrors were supposed.

Halloa! A great deal of steam! The pudding was out of the copper. A smell like a washing-day! That was the cloth. A smell like an eating-house and a pastry-cook's next door to each other, with a laundress's next door to that! That was the pudding! In half a minute Mrs Cratchit entered—flushed, but smiling proudly—with the pudding, like a speckled cannon-ball, so hard and firm, blazing in half of half a quartern of ignited brandy, and bedight with Christmas holly stuck into the top.

Oh, a wonderful pudding! Bob Cratchit said, and calmly too, that he regarded it as the greatest success achieved by Mrs Cratchit since their marriage. Mrs Cratchit said that now the weight was off her mind, she would confess she had had her doubts about the quantity of flour. Everybody had something to say about it, but nobody said or thought it was at all a small pudding for a large family. It would have been flat heresy to do so. Any Cratchit would have blushed to hint at such a thing.

At last the dinner was all done, the cloth was cleared, the hearth swept, and the fire made up. The compound in the jug being tasted, and considered perfect, apples and oranges were put upon the table, and a shovelful of chestnuts on the fire. Then all the Cratchit family drew round the hearth in what Bob Cratchit called a circle, meaning half a one; and at Bob Cratchit's elbow stood the family display of glass. Two tumblers, and a custard-cup without a handle.

These held the hot stuff from the jug, however, as well as golden goblets would have done; and Bob served it out with beaming looks, while the chestnuts on the fire sputtered and

cracked noisily. Then Bob proposed:
    'A Merry Christmas to us all, my dears. God bless us!'
    Which all the family re-echoed.
    'God bless us every one!' said Tiny Tim, the last of all.

from *A Christmas Carol*

Blow, Blow, Thou Winter Wind
William Shakespeare

Blow, blow, thou winter wind,
Thou art not so unkind
  As man's ingratitude;
Thy tooth is not so keen,
Because thou art not seen,
  Although thy breath be rude.

Heigh-ho! sing, heigh-ho! unto the green holly:
Most friendship is feigning, most loving mere folly.
  Then heigh-ho! the holly!
  This life is most jolly.

Freeze, freeze, thou bitter sky,
That dost not bite so nigh
  As benefits forgot:
Though thou the waters warp,[1]
Thy sting is not so sharp
  As friend remember'd not.

Heigh-ho! sing, heigh-ho! unto the green holly:
Most friendship is feigning, most loving mere folly.
  Then heigh-ho! the holly!
  This life is most jolly.

from *As You Like It*

[1] Harden.

114

Snow and Sun
Traditional

White bird, featherless,
Flew from Paradise,
Pitched on the castle wall;
Along came Lord Landless,
Took it up handless,
And rode away horseless to the King's white hall.

The Shepherds
Adapted by Alexander Franklin

This is part of an old play called *The Chester Miracle Play* about the shepherds going to Bethlehem. When the Angel appears, they cannot understand him because he speaks in Latin. In the earlier part of the play the shepherds, whose names are Hankin, Sym, Tud and Trowle, boast about their skill in minding sheep. Then they have a meal on the hillside and next a wrestling contest. Suddenly they are interrupted by the appearance of a bright star.

A bright star appears.

HANKIN   What is this light here
That shines so bright here
    On my black beard?
Seeing this sight here,
A man may take fright here,
    And I am afeared.

SYM   Afeared here to stay now,
I would away now
    Far from this sight.
In truth to say now,
It seems like day now,
    Yet still it is night.

TUD   On such a bright beaming
And a light gleaming
    I dare not gaze.
Brightness past dreaming
From a star streaming.
    A sight to amaze!

TROWLE   That star in the height,
I will gaze on this night,
    'Till my sight fail.
Great God in his might
Is ashine in that light,
    And good must prevail.

SYM   Fellows, all three,
Kneel down on this lea
    And calm we these fears.
Pray God with us be
And grant we may see
    Why this star appears.

TUD O Lord, hear our prayer;
    Be pleased us to spare,
     If it by thy will.
    And well may we fare,
    Though this light so rare
     Doth shine on our hill.

HANKIN Now marvel we may
    How it is like day
     As never befell.
    Therefore, I thee pray
    The truth to us say
     What these wonders foretell.

An ANGEL *appears and sings,* 'Gloria in excelsis deo et in terra pax hominibus bonæ voluntatis.' *Then he goes away, leaving the* SHEPHERDS *bewildered.*

HANKIN Fellows, I heard a wondrous song.

SYM   A song about some 'glere' or 'glore'?

TUD Nay, it was 'glory'; thou art wrong.
    I was afeared, yet would hear more.

HANKIN He sang some 'glorum' with a 'glow'.

TUD   Nay, it was 'glory'. List to me;
    I am the eldest and I know.

SYM   Nay, 'glorum, glarum' with a 'glee'.

TROWLE Nay, he sang 'glorious' say I.

HANKIN   Nay, 'glorum, glorum', like a peal.

SYM   By my faith, it was some spy
                Come cunningly, our sheep to steal.

HANKIN   Perchance 'twas Gabriel who sang.

TUD   And he sang 'glory' best by far.

TROWLE   But heard you how his 'celsis' rang,
                As well as 'bonny', 'pax', and 'tar'?

HANKIN   No singer ever sang so well;
                His 'pax' did pierce my bosom through.

SYM   'Hominibus' his song did tell,
                And 'bony voluntatis', too.

TUD   A 'terra' I did surely hear,
                Ere that bright being did depart.

TROWLE   Of 'deo' he did sing full clear;
                It was a note to heal the heart.

The ANGEL *appears again and speaks to the* SHEPHERDS.
ANGEL   Fear not Heaven's light!
                This star in the height
                Shall guide you aright,
                Till you Bethlehem find.
                For there, through God's might,
                Is Christ born this night,
                With evil to fight
                    And to save all mankind.

The ANGEL *disappears.*
HANKIN   No longer need we be afraid.
                Now forth to Bethlehem we wend

To find the place where Christ is laid,
　　Led by the star that God doth send.

TROWLE　　A song! A song! Now let us see
　　What chant will show how we rejoice.
Now all men take your time from me
　　And sing full loud with heart and voice.

TROWLE *leads the* SHEPHERDS *and all people watching the play in
a joyful song. During the singing, the* SHEPHERDS *walk about as
if making their way to Bethlehem, and when they stop they have come
to the stable. Within are* MARY *and* JOSEPH; JESUS *lies in the
manger. The* SHEPHERDS *do not notice* JOSEPH.

TUD　　The star stands in the heavens clear.
Stay we our steps; the place is near.
And we shall find our Saviour here,
　　As Gabriel did say.

HANKIN　　In truth, we have not been beguiled,
For look, Sym, here is Mary mild
And Jesu Christ, the holy child,
　　Softly lapped in hay.

SYM　　Unworthy though we men may be
Our Saviour Christ on Earth to see,
Kneel we here and pray that he
　　May grant us Heaven's crown.

The SHEPHERDS *go closer to the* HOLY FAMILY *and kneel down.*

TUD　　Now all our woe is turned to bliss,
And thank we God who hath wrought this.
Christ, our dear Lord, we would kiss
　　Thy cradle or thy gown.

TROWLE　　So rare a sight I never saw.

119

Unworthily I kneel before
My Lord, and pray that evermore
   His love on me may light.

HANKIN   Who is that grave old man who wears
About his mouth a pound of hairs?
A briar bush on his chin he bears,
   And, see, his head is white.

SYM   Since he is old, we should not jest;
For, look, his head nods to his breast.
He needs to nap and find some rest,
   As his red eyes do show.

TUD   What though his back with years be bent
And toil has all his vigour spent?
To this pure maid his care is lent:
   A worthy man I know.

MARY   Your steps my son hath led,
   And brought you to his side,
To kneel before the bed
   Where God's love doth abide.
This man hath married me,
   A virgin undefiled,
God's handmaiden to be,
   And bear this holy child.

JOSEPH   Shepherds, the law of Moses heed,
That men should wed and children breed,
And should commit no sinful deed
   Against God's holy will.
God's angel stood beside my bed
When I lay sleeping, and he said
That this pure virgin I should wed

To save her from all ill.

And now rejoice, you men of worth,
For know that God ordained this birth,
That Christ, his son, might come on Earth
    Among mankind to dwell.
Therefore, go forth and preach this thing,
And make your words with joy to ring;
For you have seen your Heavenly King,
    As prophets did foretell.

HANKIN   Great God on high, who hath made known
This wondrous thing to us alone,
Look down upon us from thy throne
    And hear our thankful prayer.

SYM   Since we be men of common sort,
The worth of these our gifts is naught.
Yet take out such as we have brought;
    Let each one give his share.

TUD   Yea, let each man do homage now.

HANKIN   Who shall go first his knee to bow?

SYM   The eldest of us all art thou,
    Therefore thy gift prepare.

HANKIN *goes up to* JESUS *and kneels.*
HANKIN   Hail, king born in a maiden's bower!
Our Saviour come in blissful hour
To fight for men the Devil's power,
    As prophets old did say.
Hail, thou King of Heaven so high,
Who in this lowly crib doth lie!

With love and reverence come I
  And to thee homage pay.
Lo, I bring to thee a bell.
I pray thee, Lord, save me from Hell,
That I may ever with thee dwell.
  And now I must away.

Having given JESUS *a bell,* HANKIN *returns to the other* SHEP-
  HERDS. SYM *goes up to* JESUS *and kneels.*

SYM   Hail, the Conqueror of Hell!
For holy prophets did foretell
That Satan and his fiends to fell
  Should be thine earthly task.
Hail, thou who made the star our guide
That led us from the far hillside!
Hail, Lord, come down on Earth to bide!
  I give thee here a flask.
And here also I give a spoon
To eat thy pottage with at noon.
Since I must take my leave full soon,
  Thy blessing now I ask.

Having given JESUS *a flask and a spoon,* SYM *returns to the others.*
  TUD *goes up to kneel before* JESUS.

TUD   Hail, the peerless Prince of Peace,
Who shall all souls from Hell release!
Rejoice we may and never cease!
  Salvation now is nigh.
Hail, Lord of Heaven, who, this morn,
To save mankind, on Earth art born!
Take here my cap; though it be worn,
  'Twill keep thee snug and dry.
For, son, I have no jewels or gold.
But this, my life, is thine to hold.
I pray thee, my poor soul enfold,

When I must come to die.

He gives JESUS *his cap and then goes back to the others.* TROWLE
takes his place, kneeling before JESUS.

TROWLE   Now, child, although thou be God's son
              And thou art with thy Father one,
              Soon shalt thou look for sweets and fun,
                 And like all children be.
              Old Joseph need not hurt his thumbs
              With picking apples, pears, and plums;
              To pull down fruit when autumn comes,
                 My nuthook I give thee.
              Though I come hindermost of all,
              And this my gift to thee is small,
              When thou shalt men to thy bliss call,
                 Good Lord, think on me.

TROWLE, *having given* JESUS *a crooked stick, returns to the others.*

HANKIN   Now, Mary, we must go our ways.
                 Farewell to thee, God's mother dear,
              Who on this wondrous day of days
                 Brought forth thy son amongst us here.
              Wherefore all men on earth shall say,
                 'Blesséd be thou in every place.'
              Keep us from stain of sin we pray,
                 To stand for ever in thy grace.

The SHEPHERDS *leave the stable.*

SYM   Brethren, let us homeward go,
                 And with loud song our Saviour praise.
              Now nought but kindness will I show.
                 And preach God's word to men always.

TUD   Over the sea, where'er men live,
                 My way leads to each foreign shore,

To preach this joy that God doth give.
A shepherd I will be no more.

TROWLE   For my misdeeds amends to make,
        Since I have seen this holy sight,
    My shepherd's craft I here forsake
        To be a holy anchorite.

HANKIN   And I a hermit, with bare feet,
        Will walk beneath the open sky;
    No more my fellow men to meet,
        But in the desert live and die.

    All worldly things I here lay down
        And think on everlasting bliss,
    That I may gain a heavenly crown.
        Now, fellows, part we with a kiss?

SYM   I yield: for since we three were boys
        We have been friends of noble worth:
    We shared our sorrows and our joys.
        Farewell! We meet no more on Earth

The SHEPHERDS *embrace and start to go their ways.*
TUD   Great God and his most precious son,
        Whose coming we go forth to tell,
    Forgive all wrongs that we have done.
        Good men, for ever, fare ye well.

TROWLE   And fare ye well, each worthy friend;
        May God his mercy show now.
    For here at last we make an end.
        Farewell! From you we go now.

TROWLE *goes out.*

The Wassail Bowl
Anonymous

The brown bowl,
The merry brown bowl,
As it goes round-about,
  Fill,
  Still,
Let the world say what it will,
And drink your fill all out.

The deep can,
The merry deep can,
As you do freely quaff
  Sing,
  Fling,
Be merry as a king,
And sound a lusty laugh.

Make We Merry
Anonymous

Make we merry, both more and less,
For now is the time of Christmas.

Let no man come into this hall,
Nor groom, nor page, nor yet marshall,
But that some sport he bring withal.

If that he say he cannot sing,
Some other sport then let him bring,
That it may please at this feasting.

If he say he naught can do,
Then, for my love, ask him no mo'
But to the stocks then let him go.

Make we merry, both more and less,
For now is the time of Christmas.

Mistletoe
Walter de la Mare

Sitting under the mistletoe
(Pale green, fairy mistletoe),
One last candle burning low,
All the sleepy dancers gone,
Just one candle burning on,
Shadows lurking everywhere:
Some one came, and kissed me there.

Tired I was; my head would go
Nodding under the mistletoe
(Pale-green, fairy mistletoe),

No footsteps came, no voice, but only,
Just as I sat there, sleepy, lonely,
Stooped in the still and shadowy air
Lips unseen—and kissed me there.

Winter
Lord Tennyson

The frost is here,
The fuel is dear,
And woods are sear,
And fires burn clear,
And frost is here
And has bitten the heel of the going year.

Bite, frost, bite!
You roll up away from the light,
The blue-wood-louse and the plump dormouse,
And the bees are stilled and the flies are killed,
And you bite far into the heart of the house,
But not into mine.

Bite, frost, bite!
The woods are all the searer,
The fuel is all the dearer,
The fires are all the clearer,
My spring is all the nearer,
You have bitten into the heart of the earth,
But not into mine.

Ragged Robin
James Reeves

Robin was a king of men,
A king of far renown,
But then he fell on evil days
And lost his royal crown.
Ragged Robin he was called;
He lived in ragged times,
And so to earn his livelihood
He took to making rhymes.

A score or so of ragged rhymes
He made—some good, some bad;
He sang them up and down the lanes
Till people called him mad.
They listened for Mad Robin's songs
Through all the countryside,
And when they heard his voice no more
They guessed that he had died.

Now Ragged Robin was not dead
But changed into a bird,
And every year on tile and tree
His piping voice is heard.
His breast is clad with scarlet red,
His cloak and hood are brown;

And once more he is Winter's king
Although he wears no crown.

A Christmas Visit
Mary Howitt

There was no coach, nor railroad between Wilton and the large town in which Mary lived; there was nothing better than the car and the carrier's cart for people to travel by, who had not their own carriage, and could hire one at the town. Mary and her grandmother were not too grand to ride in the car, the driver of which was well known to the dear old lady, and who was sure to take as much care of her and her little grandchild as if they had been gold from the Bank of England. Mary had ridden in this car before, and right glad was she to do so, because it took her to Wilton.

You must, therefore, fancy Mary sitting with her grandmother on the best seat in the car, the leather curtains of which are all carefully buckled down to keep out every draught, and four other inhabitants of Wilton, or one of the adjacent villages, are with them, for the car holds six, with sundry parcels and baskets, and little boxes, which people hold on their knees, and stow away behind their feet, and thus they go jogging along very bad roads, towards the familiar village of Wilton. Mary knew every inch of the road, yet for all that she peeped out of the openings of the curtains to notice the various points of their journey. There was the old mill, of which her papa and her Uncle Edward had so often told her the comical story of the old fat miller, who loved a joke, and one market-day ran a race in Derby, with a little nimble-footed tailor, and won it too, because, having a start given him on account of his size, he took his way along a narrow passage which was just at the end of their race, and so completely filled it up, by his enormous bulk, that the little man could not get past him. And there was the old Hall, where that famous dog lived, as is described in the *Boy's Country Book*, which set off with a lesser companion on a long journey to revenge some ill usage which he (the weaker dog) had received from a huge mastiff at an inn. The huge mastiff was left dead on the spot, and the two friends came home again, wearied out with their long travel.

About midway on their journey they came to a coal district, where Mary always took notice of the blackened road, and of the colliers who then, it being evening, were returning to their homes, with their grimy faces, their short flannel over-shirts, and the huge coal which many of them were carrying on their heads; it being, in that part of the country, customary to allow the men as much coal for their own use as they could carry home themselves. Right and left of the road, also, she never failed to notice the huge piles of slack or small coal which were piled up near the pit's mouth, and which in many cases were always burning. As long as Mary could remember this road, these hills of slack had been burning, and still would burn for years to come, as she was told.

As they approached Wilton they left the coal district, and came into that pleasant pastoral region which surrounded the village. In former times, however, there had been coal-pits even there. Some walls, and even houses, in the village had been thrown down in consequence of the excavations under their foundations; and in some of her grandpapa's fields were the remains of old pits, which never failed to fill her with a shuddering sort of interest, more especially as some rather dismal stories were told about them. Mary's grandfather, in his younger days, had been greatly concerned with these coal-pits; and hence it was that one little room in the house still went

by the name of the counting-house; and, from old habit, even the farming men were paid every Saturday night in this room.

We have taken a long time for this short journey, which we hope has not been found a tedious one. But now it is over. Mary and her grandmother are arrived; and Mary is once more struck by that which always strikes her at Wilton, the plenty there seems to be in that house, both to eat and to drink, and the large fires in almost every room. Coal was so plentiful there that her grandpapa had it merely for fetching, so there was a great fire in 'the little kitchen', where the farm-servants sat, and the 'big kitchen', where the women-servants, when they had time to sew for themselves, might sit, if they pleased. This was a room with a stone floor, and large dresser, and cupboards —such cupboards!—where Mary's grandmother distilled her rose and lavender waters, and mixed medicines for the poor; where she made her preserves, and her cakes; and where the pork-pies, and the mince-pies, and the custards and all the delicacies were compounded. Then there was a huge fire in the parlour, where grandpa and grandmamma sat; and if anybody was likely to come, there was another great fire made in the new dining-room; and these, to say nothing of fires in bedrooms, never failed to astonish Mary, and give her that sense of comfort which is so delightful.

Grandmamma had sent by the carrier's cart, the very day she herself came in the car, a vast quantity of groceries and fruit for the Christmas pies and merry-makings; and Mary had not been very long at Wilton, before she sat down with grandmamma to stone raisins, and peel apples, and grate nutmegs, and pick currants for the mince-pies. It was pleasant enough with such companionship; although I must confess to you that Mary was not particularly fond of any thing that belonged to cookery. The mince-pies were made; and a fresh supply of pork-pies and sausages, and huge seed cakes, plum cakes, and biscuits, for Harry and Kate, the other two grand-children, were about to arrive; and grandmamma knew what a treat some of these good things would be to them.

*　　　*　　　*

Mary's cousins were come. Mary, who was much more accustomed to the society of grown people than those of her own age, found in their companionship a novelty that was quite delightful. Harry, with the help of one of the men, and by means of a wagon-rope, fixed up a swing in the corn-chamber, where they amused themselves very often by swinging; he made a slide on the pond in the field where he and his sister, who was as great an adept in sliding as himself, undertook to teach Mary this 'delightful art', as he termed it. But poor Mary was not born to be a slider; and she felt a little mortified at the sort of quiet contempt with which they regarded her unsuccessful attempts after they had given up trying to teach her.

Harry wished for snow, and so did Kate; they wanted to build up a snowman, and to have a game at snowballing, and they had their wish. It began to fall on St Thomas's Day, which is the shortest day in the year; and the sight of this falling snow, and the prospect of the pleasure which it would afford them, kept Harry and Kate in a state of delightful excitement all day. Mary had an excitement, or rather a quiet, heart-felt pleasure of another kind.

Her grandpapa, who was the proprietor of a good deal of land about the village, was obliged, according to old usage, to give certain sums of money to the poor of the parish; these were called doles; one of these doles, or gifts, was given on St Thomas's Day; all of them, indeed, were given during the winter season, because then, it is supposed, that the poor suffer most. It was a dole of ten pounds, and was given to the poor, deserving widows of the parish. Mary had once before been there on a similar occasion, and her grandpapa allowed her to be the dispenser of his bounty; now she asked for the same favour, and it was cheerfully granted.

At eleven o'clock, therefore, in the morning, you must fancy 'grandpapa and grandmamma at Wilton', sitting in two large chairs, side by side, for he always would have his wife with him on these occasions, because she knew the poor so much better than he did. There they sit side by side in two old-fashioned chairs by the great kitchen fire, and, as they sit there, they look like an old Saxon king and queen. The grandfather has a canvas bag of silver coin on his knee, and a paper in his hand, to which he refers from time to time, to see who are his old pensioners, and what was their state in the former year; and after a moment's consideration, in which his wife is often referred to, Mary is told the sum of money to be given, and this she takes out of the bag.

All the time, as I tell you, this old Saxon king and queen were sitting in their great chairs the snow was falling, falling, falling; and Harry and Kate were out in the garden, snowy as it was, essaying their first game of snowballing. Their laughter and merriment came out of the snowy garden into the great kitchen, and by dinnertime, having thoroughly enjoyed them-selves, and having commenced rolling huge balls of snow for the foundation of a snowman, and then, having changed their shoes and stockings, which were soaked with snow-water, they sat down to the dinner table with faces so rosy that I know not what to compare them to; with appetites that seemed almost unappeasable, and spirits so exhilarated that they almost deafened with their merriment.

It snowed all that night, and the next morning when they woke, behold! there had not been such a fall of snow for twenty years. It lay everywhere a yard thick; and in many places, where it had been driven by the wind, several yards. The village street was one mass of snow, which the villagers were looking at, from door to window, in utter amazement, before they began to cut a way through it. Harry was overjoyed at the sight; he sprang from bed, dressed hastily, and rushed down stairs to dig away on his own account, or to help anyone else. The farm-servants had now plenty to do, for the horses were snowed up in the stables; the cows in the cow-house; the pigs in the stye, and the poultry in the hen-house; to say nothing of the dog, whose kennel was under the steps of the horse-block, so that he and his house were buried together. A road had to be cut to all these imprisoned creatures; and the small flock of sheep, in the little meadow below the orchard, had to be looked after, perhaps dug out. The well was snowed up, and so was the dairy door, and the steps which led down to the coal cellar.

Harry thought it was the most amusing thing in the world, and he was instantly at work with the men, shovelling and singing with all his might; it was wonderful that he had breath for both. Kate was not long after him; and then she might be seen with her frock pinned up, great over-boots on, and a woollen shawl tied over her head, but to some little disadvantage, because every thing in the shape of a spade was already in the hands of man or boy, and she had nothing better than the kitchen fire-shovel to work with.

This was on the Wednesday; Christmas Day was on the Sunday this year. Mary's father and mother were to come on Saturday for Christmas Eve, and to spend several days of the following Christmas week at Wilton; now she feared that the great snow would prevent this, more especially as they heard that the road was impassable all the way. Plenty of people beside Mary had similar fears, and the different parishes therefore sent out poor men by hundreds, to open the roads, for which they received good wages, and work thus coming unexpectedly, at a season when so many were unemployed, it was thought quite a blessing to the poor.

Christmas Eve was come. Holly and mistletoe decorated the house; a huge kissing-bunch was suspended from the ceiling of the great kitchen, where, on that evening, there were to be all sorts of games, and to partake of which at least a dozen children were invited. Spite of the snow Mary's parents arrived, and so did Uncle Edward.

I need not tell you all the games that were played; hunt the slipper, blind-man's buff, turn the trencher, and suchlike, in which the grown-up people, as well as the children, took part. I need not tell you of the great yule log, nor the huge brown-posset pot, which held several quarts of ale-posset, of which, according to custom, everybody, old and young, must partake; nor of the old fiddler who came in and played while they danced; nor of the songs that were sung, in which Harry cut a capital figure, nor of the stories that were told; nor of the jokes and merriment that there were. You have all of you, no doubt, spent a Christmas Eve in a farmhouse, and in that case you know all the fun, and can imagine what a beautiful supper there was in the new 'dining-room', where another great log was burning; and can taste, in imagination, the hot turkey, the mince-pies, the custards, the cakes, the apples, the nuts, and all the other good things.

They sat up playing games, and guessing riddles, and telling many stories till midnight, when the carol singers came round with a band of music, and then they were all silent to listen. It was a beautiful winter's night; the stars shone out by thousands in the sky; and the earth below was clothed with its unbroken covering of pure snow, which having frozen, was now as hard as a marble pavement. They sang the old-fashioned carol of—

> Christians, awake, salute the happy morn,
> On which the Saviour of mankind was born.

And Mary, who had a deal of poetical feeling, thought it was the most beautiful music she had ever heard.

That was a delightful Christmas Eve. It was Christmas Day; a splendid winter's morning; the sun shone, and the frozen snow seemed full of little diamonds. As soon as breakfast was over they set out to the little old-fashioned chapel, at about three miles' distance. Mary was to ride the pony which she had at Linford, and which was now always called hers; the grandpapa also rode on his tall, stout horse, and when he was mounted he looked, as he sat on the horse, in his large ample coat and old-fashioned hat, like that same old Saxon king of whom I spoke before, mounted and ready to ride to some Wittenagemot, or meeting of the aldermen. Away trotted grandpapa, and Mary cantered by his side; and grandmamma, and Harry, and Kate came trotting after in the gig; Harry being privileged to drive. Besides those who rode and drove, there were three who walked, Mary's father and mother, and Uncle Edward, who set off half an hour before the others.

Mary, as she went along, was reminded continuously of the northern regions; their way lay along narrow roads through which a path had been cut in the snow, and which now was well-tracked. The snow lay halfway up the hedges, and loaded the branches of the trees as with a new foliage, and bowed them down like an arch above the road, casting over all a sort of twilight gloom. The fields lay like one immense plain, for where the hedges were low they were completely buried. All was as still and hushed as in a dream; the only sound that came clearly to the ear were the church bells, which now, more than ever, seemed to descend from heaven. The little chapel, to which they were going, stood on the ridge of a lofty stretch of country, and was seen at a great distance; a number of fir trees which surrounded it stood up aloft, at all times, like a land-mark, but were now, more than ever, made visible by the contrast of colour. At every turn of the road, wherever there had been an eddy of wind, the snow had been driven into huge heaps, and scooped out, as it were, into caves, the roofs of which seemed to hang over in the most graceful curves and scrolls.

It was a delightful ride.

A Ballad of Christmas
Walter de la Mare

It was about the deep of night,
　And still was earth and sky,
When in the moonlight, dazzling bright,
　Three ghosts came riding by.

Beyond the sea—beyond the sea,
　Lie kingdoms for them all:
I wot their steeds trod wearily—
　The journey is not small.

By rock and desert, sand and stream,
　They footsore late did go:
Now, like a sweet and blessed dream,
　Their path was deep with snow.

Shining like hoar-frost, rode they on,
　Three ghosts in earth's array:
It was about the hour when wan
　Night turns at hint of day.

For bloody was each hand, and dark
  With death each orbless eye;—
It was three Traitors mute and stark
  Came riding silent by.

Silver their raiment and their spurs,
  And silver-shod their feet,
And silver-pale each face that stared
  Into the moonlight sweet.

And he upon the left that rode
  Was Pilate, Prince of Rome,
Whose journey once lay far abroad,
  And now was nearing home.

And he upon the right that rode,
  Herod of Salem sate,
Whose mantle dipped in children's blood
  Shone clear as Heaven's gate.

And he, these twain betwixt, that rode
  Was clad as white as wool,
Dyed in the Mercy of his God,
  White was he crown to sole.

Throned 'mid a myriad Saints in bliss
  Rise shall the Babe of Heaven
To shine on these three ghosts, iwis,
  Smit through with sorrows seven;

Babe of the Blessed Trinity
  Shall smile their steeds to see:
Herod and Pilate riding by,
  And Judas, one of three.

Bread and Milk
Christina Rossetti

Bread and milk for breakfast,
    And woollen frocks to wear,
And a crumb for Robin Redbreast
    On the cold days of the year.

The Thames Frozen January 1684
John Evelyn

The frost continuing more and more severe, the Thames before
London was still planted with booths in formal streets, all
sorts of trades and shops furnished, and full of commodities,
even to a printing press, where the people and ladies took a
fancy to have their names printed, and the day and year set
down when printed on the Thames: this humour took so
universally that it was estimated the printer gained £5 a day
for printing a line only, at sixpence a name, besides what he
got by ballads, &c. Coaches plied from Westminster to the
Temple, and from several other stairs to and fro, as in the
streets, sleds, sliding with skates, a bull-baiting, horse and

coach-races, puppet-plays and interludes, cooks, tippling, and other lewd places, so that it seemed to be a bacchanalian triumph, or carnival on the water, whilst it was a severe judgment on the land, the trees not only splitting, as if lightning-struck, but men and cattle perishing in divers places, and the very seas so locked up with ice, that no vessel could stir out or come in. The fowls, fish and birds, and all our exotic plants and greens, universally perishing. Many parks of deer were destroyed, and all sorts of fuel so dear, that there were great contributions to preserve the poor alive.

Frost
Arthur Ransome

Once upon a time there were an old man and an old woman. Now the old woman was the old man's second wife. His first wife had died, and had left him with a little daughter: Martha she was called. Then he married again, and God gave him a cross wife, and with her two more daughters, and they were very different from the first.

The old woman loved her own daughters, and gave them red kisel jelly every day, and honey too, as much as they could put into their greedy little mouths. But poor little Martha, the eldest, she got only what the others left. When they were cross they threw away what they left, and then she got nothing at all.

The children grew older, and the step-mother made Martha do all the work of the house. She had to fetch the wood for the stove, and light it and keep it burning. She had to draw the water for her sisters to wash their hands in. She had to make the clothes, and wash them and mend them. She had to cook the dinner, and clean the dishes after the others had done before having a bite for herself.

For all that the step-mother was never satisfied, and was for ever shouting at her: 'Look, the kettle is in the wrong place;' 'There is dust on the floor;' 'There is a spot on the tablecloth;' or, 'The spoons are not clean, you stupid, ugly, idle hussy.' But Martha was not idle. She worked all day long, and got up before the sun, while her sisters never stirred from their beds till it was time for dinner. And she was not stupid. She always had a song on her lips, except when her step-mother had beaten her. And as for being ugly, she was the prettiest little girl in the village.

Her father saw all this, but he could not do anything, for the old woman was mistress at home, and he was terribly afraid of her. And as for the daughters, they saw how their mother treated Martha, and they did the same. They were always complaining and getting her into trouble. It was a pleasure to them to see the tears on her pretty cheeks.

Well, time went on, and the little girl grew up, and the daughters of the stepmother were as ugly as could be. Their eyes were always cross, and their mouths were always complaining. Their mother saw that no one would want to marry either of them while there was Martha about the house, with her bright eyes and her songs and her kindness to everybody.

So she thought of a way to get rid of her step-daughter, and a cruel way it was.

'See here, old man,' says she, 'it is high time Martha was married, and I have a bridegroom in mind for her. Tomorrow morning you must harness the old mare to the sledge, and put a bit of food together and be ready to start early, as I'd like to see you back before night.'

To Martha she said: 'Tomorrow you must pack your things in a box, and put on your best dress to show yourself to your betrothed.'

'Who is he?' asked Martha with red cheeks.

'You will know when you see him,' said the step-mother.

All that night Martha hardly slept. She could hardly believe that she was really going to escape from the old woman at last, and have a hut of her own, where there would be no one to scold her. She wondered who the young man was. She hoped he was Fedor Ivanovitch, who had such kind eyes, and such nimble fingers on the balalaika, and such a merry way of flinging out his heels when he danced the Russian dance. But although he always smiled at her when they met, she felt she hardly dared to hope that it was he. Early in the morning she got up and said her prayers to God, put the whole hut in order, and packed her things into a little box. That was easy, because she had such few things. It was the other daughters who had new dresses. Any old thing was good enough for Martha. But she put on her best blue dress, and there she was, as pretty a little maid as ever walked under the birch trees in spring.

The old man harnessed the mare to the sledge and brought it to the door. The snow was very deep and frozen hard, and the wind peeled the skin from his ears before he covered them with the flaps of his fur hat.

'Sit down at the table and have a bite before you go,' says the old woman.

The old man sat down, and his daughter with him, and drank a glass of tea and ate some black bread. And the old woman put some cabbage soup, left from the day before, in a saucer, and said to Martha, 'Eat this, my little pigeon, and get ready for the road.' But when she said 'my little pigeon', she did not smile with her eyes, but only with her cruel mouth, and Martha was afraid. The old woman whispered to the old man: 'I have a word for you, old fellow. You will take Martha to her betrothed, and I'll tell you the way. You go straight along, and then take the road to the right into the forest . . . you know . . . straight to the big fir tree that stands on a hillock, and there

144

you will give Martha to her betrothed and leave her. He will be waiting for her, and his name is Frost.'

The old man stared, opened his mouth, and stopped eating. The little maid, who had heard the last words, began to cry.

'Now, what are you whimpering about?' screamed the old woman. 'Frost is a rich bridegroom and a handsome one. See how much he owns. All the pines and firs are his, and the birch trees. Any one would envy his possessions, and he himself is a very bogatir,[1] a man of strength and power.'

The old man trembled, and said nothing in reply. And Martha went on crying quietly, though she tried to stop her tears. The old man packed up what was left of the black bread, told Martha to put on her sheepskin coat, set her in the sledge and climbed in, and drove off along the white, frozen road.

The road was long and the country open, and the wind grew colder and colder, while the frozen snow blew up from under the hoofs of the mare and spattered the sledge with white patches. The tale is soon told, but it takes time to happen, and the sledge was white all over long before they turned off into the forest.

They came in the end deep into the forest, and left the road, and over the deep snow through the trees to the great fir. There the old man stopped, told his daughter to get out of the sledge, set her little box under the fir, and said, 'Wait here for your bridegroom, and when he comes be sure to receive him with kind words.' Then he turned the mare round and drove home, with the tears running from his eyes and freezing on his cheeks before they had had time to reach his beard.

The little maid sat and trembled. Her sheepskin coat was worn through, and in her blue bridal dress she sat, while fits of shivering shook her whole body. She wanted to run away; but she had not strength to move, or even to keep her little white teeth from chattering between her frozen lips.

Suddenly, not far away, she heard Frost crackling among

[1] The bogatirs were strong men, heroes of old Russia.

145

the fir trees. He was leaping from tree to tree, crackling as he came.

He leapt at last into the great fir tree, under which the little maid was sitting. He crackled in the top of the tree, and then called down out of the topmost branches——

'Are you warm, little maid?'

'Warm, warm, little Father Frost.'

Frost laughed, and came a little lower in the tree and crackled and crackled louder than before. Then he asked——

'Are you still warm, little maid? Are you warm, little red cheeks?'

The little maid could hardly speak. She was nearly dead, but she answered——

'Warm, dear Frost; warm, little father.'

Frost climbed lower in the tree, and crackled louder than ever, and asked——

'Are you still warm, little maid? Are you warm, little red cheeks? Are you warm, little paws?'

The little maid was benumbed all over, but she whispered so that Frost could just hear her——

'Warm, little pigeon, warm, dear Frost.'

And Frost was sorry for her, leapt down with a tremendous crackle and a scattering of frozen snow, wrapped the little maid up in rich furs, and covered her with warm blankets.

In the morning the old woman said to her husband, 'Drive off now to the forest, and wake the young couple.'

The old man wept when he thought of his little daughter, for he was sure that he would find her dead. He harnessed the mare, and drove off through the snow. He came to the tree, and heard his little daughter singing merrily, while Frost crackled and laughed. There she was, alive and warm, with a good fur cloak about her shoulders, a rich veil, costly blankets round her feet, and a box full of splendid presents.

The old man did not say a word. He was too surprised. He just sat in the sledge staring, while the little maid lifted her box

and the box of presents, set them in the sledge, climbed in, and sat down beside him.

They came home, and the little maid, Martha, fell at the feet of her stepmother. The old woman nearly went off her head with rage when she saw her alive, with her fur cloak and rich veil, and the box of splendid presents fit for the daughter of a prince.

'Ah, you slut,' she cried, 'you won't get round me like that!'

And she would not say another word to the little maid, but went about all day long biting her nails and thinking what to do.

At night she said to the old man——

'You must take my daughters, too, to that bridegroom in the forest. He will give them better gifts than these.'

Things take time to happen, but the tale is quickly told. Early next morning the old woman woke her daughters, fed them with good food, dressed them like brides, hustled the old man, made him put clean hay in the sledge and warm blankets, and sent them off to the forest.

The old man did as he was bid—drove to the big fir tree, set the boxes under the tree, lifted out the step-daughters and set them on the boxes side by side, and drove back home.

They were warmly dressed, these two, and well fed, and at first, as they sat there, they did not think about the cold.

'I can't think what put it into mother's head to marry us both at once,' said the first, 'and to send us here to be married. As if there were not enough young men in the village. Who can tell what sort of fellows we shall meet here!'

Then they began to quarrel.

'Well,' says one of them, 'I'm beginning to get the cold shivers. If our fated ones do not come soon, we shall perish of cold.'

'It's a flat lie to say that bridegrooms get ready early. It's already dinner-time.'

'What if only one comes?'

'You'll have to come another time.'

'You think he'll look at you?'

'Well, he won't take you, anyhow.'

'Of course he'll take me.'

'Take you first! It's enough to make any one laugh!'

They began to fight and scratch each other, so that their cloaks fell open and the cold entered their bosoms.

Frost, crackling among the trees, laughing to himself, froze the hands of the two quarrelling girls, and they hid their hands in the sleeves of their fur coats and shivered, and went on scolding and jeering at each other.

'Oh, you ugly mug, dirty nose! What sort of a housekeeper will you make?'

'And what about you, boasting one? You know nothing but how to gad about and lick your own face. We'll soon see which of us he'll take.'

And the two girls went on wrangling and wrangling till they began to freeze in good earnest.

Suddenly they cried out together——

'Devil take these bridegrooms for being so long in coming! You have turned blue all over.'

And together they replied, shivering——

'No bluer than yourself, tooth-chatterer.'

And Frost, not so far away, crackled and laughed, and leapt from fir tree to fir tree, crackling as he came.

The girls heard that someone was coming through the forest.

'Listen! there's someone coming. Yes, and with bells on his sledge!'

'Shut up, you slut! I can't hear, and the frost is taking the skin off me."

They began blowing on their fingers.

And Frost came nearer and nearer, crackling, laughing, talking to himself. Nearer and nearer he came, leaping from tree-top to tree-top, till at last he leapt into the great fir under which the two girls were sitting and quarrelling.

He leant down, looking through the branches, and asked——

'Are you warm, maidens? Are you warm, little red cheeks? Are you warm, little pigeons?'

'Ugh, Frost, the cold is hurting us. We are frozen. We are waiting for our bridegrooms, but the cursed fellows have not turned up.'

Frost came a little lower in the tree, and crackled louder and swifter.

'Are you warm, maidens? Are you warm, my little red cheeks?'

'Go to the devil!' they cried out. 'Are you blind? Our hands and feet are frozen!'

Frost came still lower in the branches, and cracked and crackled louder than ever.

'Are you warm, maidens?' he asked.

'Into the pit with you, with all the fiends,' the girls screamed at him, 'you ugly, wretched fellow!' . . . And as they were cursing at him their bad words died on their lips, for the two girls, the cross children of the cruel stepmother, were frozen stiff where they sat.

Frost hung from the lowest branches of the tree, swaying and crackling while he looked at the anger frozen on their faces. Then he climbed swiftly up again, and crackling and cracking, chuckling to himself, he went off, leaping from fir tree to fir tree, this way and that through the white, frozen forest.

In the morning the old woman says to her husband——

'Now then, old man, harness the mare to the sledge, and put new hay in the sledge to be warm for my little ones, and lay fresh rushes on the hay to be soft for them; and take warm rugs with you, for maybe they will be cold, even in their furs. And look sharp about it, and don't keep them waiting. The frost is hard this morning, and it was harder in the night.'

The old man had not time to eat even a mouthful of black bread before she had driven him out into the snow. He put hay and rushes and soft blankets in the sledge, and harnessed the mare, and went off to the forest. He came to the great fir, and found the two girls sitting under it dead, with their anger still to be seen on their frozen, ugly faces.

He picked them up, first one and then the other, and put them in the rushes and the warm hay, covered them with the blankets, and drove home.

The old woman saw him coming, far away, over the shining snow. She ran to meet him, and shouted out——

'Where are the little ones?'

'In the sledge.'

She snatched off the blankets and pulled aside the rushes, and found the bodies of her two cross daughters.

Instantly she flew at the old man in a storm of rage. 'What have you done to my children, my little red cherries, my little pigeons? I will kill you with the oven fork! I will break your head with the poker!'

The old man listened till she was out of breath and could not say another word. That, my dears, is the only wise thing to do when a woman is in a scolding rage. And as soon as she had no breath left with which to answer him, he said——

'My little daughter got riches for soft words, but yours were always rough of the tongue. And it's not my fault, anyhow, for you yourself sent them into the forest.'

Well, at last the old woman got her breath again, and scolded away till she was tired out. But in the end she made her peace with the old man, and they lived together as quietly as could be expected.

As for Martha, Fedor Ivanovitch sought her in marriage, as he had meant to do all along—yes, and married her; and pretty she looked in the furs that Frost had given her. I was at the feast, and drank beer and mead with the rest. And she had the prettiest children that ever were seen—yes, and the best behaved. For if ever they thought of being naughty, the old grandfather told them the story of crackling Frost, and how kind words won kindness, and cross words cold treatment.

And mind, if ever Frost asks you if you are warm, be as polite to him as you can. And to do that, the best way is to be good always, like little Martha. Then it comes easy.

from *Old Peter's Russian Tales*

Snowing
Walter de la Mare

Snowing; snowing;
Oh, between earth and sky
A wintry wind is blowing,
Scattering with its sigh
Petals from trees of silver that shine
Like invisible glass, when the moon
In the void of night on high
Paces her orchards divine.

Snowing; snowing;
Ah me, how still, and how fair
The air with flakes interflowing,
The fields crystal and bare,
When the brawling brooks are dumb
And the parched trees matted with frost,
And the birds in this wilderness stare
Dazzled and num'd!

Snowing . . . snowing . . . snowing:
Moments of time through space
Into hours, centuries growing,

Till the world's marred lovely face,
Wearied of change and chance,
Radiant in innocent dream—
Lulled by an infinite grace
To rest in eternal trance.

Christmas
Michael Bond

Paddington found that Christmas took a long time to come. Each morning when he hurried downstairs he crossed the date off the calendar, but the more days he crossed off the farther away it seemed.

However, there was plenty to occupy his mind. For one thing, the postman started arriving later and later in the morning, and when he did finally reach the Browns' house there were so many letters to deliver he had a job to push them all through the letter-box. Often there were mysterious-looking parcels as well, which Mrs Bird promptly hid before Paddington had time to squeeze them.

A surprising number of the envelopes were addressed to Paddington himself, and he carefully made a list of all those who had sent him Christmas cards so that he could be sure of thanking them.

'You may be only a small bear,' said Mrs Bird, as she helped him arrange the cards on the mantelpiece, 'but you certainly leave your mark.'

Paddington wasn't sure how to take this, especially as Mrs

Bird had just polished the hall floor, but when he examined his paws they were quite clean.

Paddington had made his own Christmas cards. Some he had drawn himself, decorating the edges with holly and mistletoe; others had been made out of pictures cut from Mrs Brown's magazines. But each one had the words A MERRY CHRISTMAS AND A HAPPY NEW YEAR printed on the front, and they were signed PADINGTUN BROWN on the inside—together with his special paw mark to show that they were genuine.

Paddington wasn't sure about the spelling of A MERRY CHRISTMAS. It didn't look at all right. But Mrs Bird checked all the words in a dictionary for him to make certain.

'I don't suppose many people get Christmas cards from a bear,' she explained. 'They'll probably want to keep them, so you ought to make sure they are right.'

One evening Mr Brown arrived home with a huge Christmas tree tied to the roof of his car. It was placed in a position of honour by the dining-room window and both Paddington and Mr Brown spent a long time decorating it with coloured electric lights and silver tinsel.

Apart from the Christmas tree, there were paper chains and holly to be put up, and large coloured bells made of crinkly paper. Paddington enjoyed doing the paper chains. He managed to persuade Mr Brown that bears were very good at putting up decorations and together they did most of the house, with Paddington standing on Mr Brown's shoulders while Mr Brown handed up the drawing pins. It came to an unhappy end one evening when Paddington accidentally put his paw on a drawing pin which he'd left on top of Mr Brown's head. When Mrs Bird rushed into the dining-room to see what all the fuss was about, and to inquire why all the lights had suddenly gone out, she found Paddington hanging by his paws from the chandelier and Mr Brown dancing round the room rubbing his head.

But by then the decorations were almost finished and the

house had taken on quite a festive air. The sideboard was groaning under the weight of nuts and oranges, dates and figs, none of which Paddington was allowed to touch, and Mr Brown had stopped smoking his pipe and was filling the air instead with the smell of cigars.

The excitement in the Browns' house mounted, until it reached fever pitch a few days before Christmas, when Jonathan and Judy arrived home for the holidays.

But if the days leading up to Christmas were busy and exciting, they were nothing compared with Christmas Day itself.

The Browns were up early on Christmas morning—much earlier than they had intended. It all started when Paddington

woke to find a large pillow case at the bottom of his bed. His
eyes nearly popped out with astonishment when he switched
his torch on, for it was bulging with parcels, and it certainly
hadn't been there when he'd gone to bed on Christmas Eve.

Paddington's eyes grew larger and larger as he unwrapped
the brightly coloured paper round each present. A few days
before, on Mrs Bird's instructions, he had made a list of all the
things he hoped to have given him and had hidden it up one
of the chimneys. It was a strange thing, but everything on that
list seemed to be in the pillow case.

There was a large chemistry outfit from Mr Brown, full of
jars and bottles and test tubes, which looked very interesting.
And there was a miniature xylophone from Mrs Brown, which
pleased him no end. Paddington was fond of music—especially
the loud sort, which was good for conducting—and he had
always wanted something he could actually play.

Mrs Bird's parcel was even more exciting, for it contained
a checked cap which he'd especially asked for and had under-
lined on his list. Paddington stood on the end of his bed,
admiring the effect in the mirror for quite a while.

Jonathan and Judy had each given him a travel book. Paddington was very interested in geography, being a much-travelled bear, and he was pleased to see there were plenty of maps and coloured pictures inside.

The noise from Paddington's room was soon sufficient to waken both Jonathan and Judy, and in no time at all the whole house was in an uproar, with wrapping paper and bits of string everywhere.

'I'm as patriotic as the next man,' grumbled Mr Brown. 'But I draw the line when bears start playing the National Anthem at six o'clock in the morning—especially on a xylophone.'

As always, it was left to Mrs Bird to restore order. 'No more presents until after lunch,' she said, firmly. She had just tripped over Paddington on the upstairs landing, where he was investigating his new chemical outfit, and something nasty had gone in one of her slippers.

'It's all right, Mrs Bird,' said Paddington, consulting his instruction book, 'it's only some iron filings. I don't think they're dangerous.'

'Dangerous or not,' said Mrs Bird, 'I've a big dinner to cook —not to mention your birthday cake to finish decorating.'

Being a bear, Paddington had two birthdays each year— one in the summer and one at Christmas—and the Browns were holding a party in his honour to which Mr Gruber had been invited.

After they'd had breakfast and been to church, the morning passed quickly and Paddington spent most of his time trying to decide what to do next. With so many things from which to choose it was most difficult. He read some chapters from his books and made several interesting smells and a small explosion with his chemical outfit.

Mr Brown was already in trouble for having given it to him, especially when Paddington found a chapter in the instruction book headed 'Indoor Fireworks.' He made himself a 'never ending' snake which wouldn't stop growing and frightened Mrs Bird to death when she met it coming down the stairs.

'If we don't watch out,' she confided to Mrs Brown, 'we shan't last over Christmas. We shall either be blown to smithereens or poisoned. He was testing my gravy with some litmus paper just now.'

Mrs Brown sighed. 'It's a good job Christmas only comes once a year,' she said, as she helped Mrs Bird with the potatoes.

'It isn't over yet,' warned Mrs Bird.

Fortunately, Mr Gruber arrived at that moment and some measure of order was established before they all sat down to dinner.

Paddington's eyes glistened as he surveyed the table. He didn't agree with Mr Brown when he said it all looked too good to eat. All the same, even Paddington got noticeably slower towards the end when Mrs Bird brought in the Christmas pudding.

'Well,' said Mr Gruber, a few minutes later, as he sat back and surveyed his empy plate, 'I must say that's the best Christmas dinner I've had for many a day. Thank you very much indeed!'

'Hear! Hear' agreed Mr Brown. 'What do you say, Paddington?'

'It was very nice,' said Paddington, licking some cream from his whiskers. 'Except I had a bone in my Christmas pudding.'

'You *what?*' exclaimed Mrs Brown. 'Don't be silly—there are no bones in Christmas pudding.'

'I had one,' said Paddington, firmly. 'It was all hard—and it stuck in my throat.'

'Good gracious!' exclaimed Mrs Bird. 'The sixpence! I always put a piece of silver in the Christmas pudding.'

'What!' said Paddington, nearly falling off his chair. 'A sixpence? I've never heard of a sixpence pudding before.'

'Quick,' shouted Mr Brown, rising to the emergency. 'Turn him upside down.'

Before Paddington could reply, he found himself hanging head downwards while Mr Brown and Mr Gruber took it in turns to shake him. The rest of the family stood round watching the floor.

'It's no good,' said Mr Brown, after a while. 'It must have

gone too far.' He helped Mr Gruber lift Paddington into an armchair where he lay gasping for breath.

'I've got a magnet upstairs,' said Jonathan. 'We could try lowering it down his throat on a piece of string.'

'I don't think so, dear,' said Mrs Brown, in a worried tone of voice. 'He might swallow that and then we should be even worse off.' She bent over the chair. 'How do you feel, Paddington?'

'Sick,' said Paddington, in an aggrieved tone of voice.

'Of course you do, dear,' said Mrs Brown. 'It's only to be expected. There's only one thing to do—we shall have to send for the doctor.'

'Thank goodness I scrubbed it first,' said Mrs Bird. 'It might have been covered with germs.'

'But I *didn't* swallow it,' gasped Paddington. 'I only nearly did. Then I put it on the side of my plate. I didn't know it was a sixpence because it was all covered with Christmas pudding.'

Paddington felt very fed up. He'd just eaten one of the best dinners he could ever remember and now he'd been turned upside down and shaken without even being given time to explain.

Everyone exchanged glances and then crept quietly away,

leaving Paddington to recover by himself. There didn't seem to be much they *could* say.

But after the dinner things had been cleared away, and by the time Mrs Bird had made some strong coffee, Paddington was almost himself again. He was sitting up in the chair helping himself to some dates when they trooped back into the room. It took a lot to make Paddington ill for very long.

When they had finished their coffee, and were sitting round the blazing fire feeling warm and comfortable, Mr Brown rubbed his hands. 'Now, Paddington,' he said, 'it's not only Christmas, it's your birthday as well. What would you like to do?'

A mysterious expression came over Paddington's face. 'If you all go in the other room,' he announced, 'I've a special surprise for you.'

'Oh dear, *must* we, Paddington?' said Mrs Brown. 'There isn't a fire.'

'I shan't be long,' said Paddington, firmly. 'But it's a special surprise and it has to be prepared.' He held the door open and the Browns, Mrs Bird and Mr Gruber filed obediently into the other room.

'Now close your eyes,' said Paddington, when they were all settled, 'and I'll let you know when I'm ready.'

Mrs Brown shivered. 'I hope you won't be too long,' she called. But the only reply was the sound of the door clicking shut.

They waited for several minutes without speaking, and then Mr Gruber cleared his throat. 'Do you think young Mr Brown's forgotten about us?' he asked.

'I don't know,' said Mrs Brown. 'But I'm not waiting much longer.'

'Henry!' she exclaimed, as she opened her eyes. 'Have you gone to sleep?'

'Er, wassat?' snorted Mr Brown. He had eaten such a large dinner he was finding it difficult to keep awake. 'What's happening? Have I missed anything?'

'Nothing's happening,' said Mrs Brown. 'Henry, you'd better go and see what Paddington's up to.'

Several more minutes went by before Mr Brown returned to announce that he couldn't find Paddington anywhere.

'Well, he must be *somewhere*,' said Mrs Brown. 'Bears don't disappear into thin air.'

'Crikey!' exclaimed Jonathan, as a thought suddenly struck him. 'You don't think he's playing at Father Christmas, do you? He was asking all about it the other day when he put his list up the chimney. I bet that's why he wanted us to come in here—because this chimney connects with the one upstairs— and there isn't a fire.'

'Father Christmas?' said Mr Brown. 'I'll give him Father Christmas!' He stuck his head up the chimney and called Paddington's name several times. 'I can't see anything,' he said, striking a match. As if in answer a large lump of soot descended and burst on top of his head.

'Now look what you've done, Henry,' said Mrs Brown. 'Shouting so—you've disturbed the soot. All over your clean shirt!'

'If it *is* young Mr Brown, perhaps he's stuck somewhere,' suggested Mr Gruber. 'He did have rather a large dinner. I remember wondering at the time where he put it all.'

Mr Gruber's suggestion had an immediate effect on the party and everyone began to look serious.

'Why, he might suffocate with the fumes,' exclaimed Mrs Bird, as she hurried outside to the broom cupboard.

When she returned, armed with a mop, everyone took it in turns to poke it up the chimney but even though they strained their ears they couldn't hear a sound.

It was while the excitement was at its height that Paddington came into the room. He looked most surprised when he saw Mr Brown with his head up the chimney.

'You can come into the dining-room now,' he announced, looking round the room. 'I've finished wrapping my presents and they're all on the Christmas tree.'

'You don't mean to say,' spluttered Mr Brown, as he sat in the fireplace rubbing his face with a handkerchief, 'you've been in the other room all the time?'

'Yes,' said Paddington, innocently. 'I hope I didn't keep you waiting too long.'

Mrs Brown looked at her husband. 'I thought you said you'd looked everywhere,' she exclaimed.

'Well—we'd just come from the dining-room,' said Mr Brown, looking very sheepish. 'I didn't think he'd be *there*.'

'It only goes to show,' said Mrs Bird hastily, as she caught sight of the expression on Mr Brown's face, 'how easy it it to give a bear a bad name.'

Paddington looked most interested when they explained to him what all the fuss was about.

'I never thought of coming down the chimney,' he said, staring at the fireplace.

'Well, you're not thinking about it now either,' replied Mr Brown, sternly.

But even Mr Brown's expression changed as he followed Paddington into the dining-room and saw the surprise that had been prepared for them.

In addition to the presents that had already been placed on the tree, there were now six newly wrapped ones tied to the lower branches. If the Browns recognized the wrapping paper they had used for Paddington's presents earlier in the day, they were much too polite to say anything.

'I'm afraid I had to use old paper,' said Paddington apologetically, as he waved a paw at the tree. 'I hadn't any money left. That's why you had to go in the other room while I wrapped them.'

'Really, Paddington,' said Mrs Brown. 'I'm very cross with you—spending all your money on presents for us.'

'I'm afraid they're rather ordinary,' said Paddington, as he settled back in a chair to watch the others. 'But I hope you like them. They're all labelled so that you know which is which.'

'Ordinary?' exclaimed Mr Brown, as he opened his parcel. 'I don't call a pipe rack ordinary. And there's an ounce of my favourite tobacco tied to the back as well!'

'Gosh! A new stamp album!' cried Jonathan. 'Whizzo! And it's got some stamps inside already.'

'They're Peruvian ones from Aunt Lucy's postcards,' said Paddington. 'I've been saving them for you.'

'And I've got a box of paints,' exclaimed Judy. 'Thank you very much, Paddington. It's just what I wanted.'

'We all seem to be lucky,' said Mrs Brown, as she unwrapped a parcel containing a bottle of her favourite lavender water. 'How *did* you guess? I finished my last bottle only a week ago.'

'I'm sorry about your parcel, Mrs Bird,' said Paddington, looking across the room. 'I had a bit of a job with the knots.'

'It must be something special,' said Mr Brown. 'It seems all string and no parcel.'

'That's because it's really clothes line,' explained Paddington, 'not string. I rescued it when I got stuck in the revolving door at Crumbold and Ferns.'

'That makes two presents in one,' said Mrs Bird, as she freed the last of the knots and began unwinding yards and yards of paper. 'How exciting. I can't think what it can be.'

'Why,' she exclaimed. 'I do believe its a brooch! And it's shaped like a bear—how lovely!' Mrs Bird looked most touched as she handed the present round for everyone to see. 'I shall keep it in a safe place,' she added, 'and only wear it on special occasions—when I want to impress people.'

'I don't know what mine is,' said Mr Gruber, as they all turned to him. He squeezed the parcel. 'It's such a funny shape.'

'It's a drinking mug!' he exclaimed, his face lighting up with pleasure. 'And it even has my name painted on the side!'

'It's for your elevenses, Mr Gruber,' said Paddington. 'I noticed your old one was getting rather chipped.'

'I'm sure it will make my cocoa taste better than it ever has before,' said Mr Gruber.

He stood up and cleared his throat. 'I think I would like to offer a vote of thanks to young Mr Brown,' he said, 'for all his nice presents. I'm sure he must have given them a great deal of thought.'

'Hear! Hear!' echoed Mr Brown, as he filled his pipe.

Mr Gruber felt under his chair. 'And while I think of it, Mr Brown, I have a small present for you.'

Everyone stood round and watched while Paddington struggled with his parcel, eager to see what Mr Gruber had bought him. A gasp of surprise went up as he tore the paper to one side, for it was a beautifully bound leather scrapbook, with 'Paddington Brown' printed in gold leaf on the cover.

Paddington didn't know what to say, but Mr Gruber waved his thanks to one side. 'I know how you enjoy writing about your adventures, Mr Brown,' he said. 'And you have so many. I'm sure your present scrapbook must be almost full.'

'It is,' said Paddington, earnestly. 'And I'm sure I shall have lots more. Things happen to me, you know. But I shall only put my best ones in here!'

When he made his way up to bed later that evening, his mind was in such a whirl, and he was so full of good things, he could hardly climb the stairs—let alone think about anything. He wasn't quite sure which he had enjoyed most. The presents, the Christmas dinner, the games, or the tea—with the special marmalade-layer birthday cake Mrs Bird had made in his honour. Pausing on the corner half-way up, he decided he had enjoyed giving his own presents best of all.

'Paddington! Whatever have you got there?' He jumped and hastily hid his paw behind his back as he heard Mrs Bird calling from the bottom of the stairs.

'It's only some sixpence pudding, Mrs Bird,' he called, looking over the banisters guiltily. 'I thought I might get hungry during the night and I didn't want to take any chances.'

'Honestly!' Mrs Bird exclaimed, as she was joined by the others. 'What *does* that bear look like? A paper hat about ten sizes too big on his head—Mr Gruber's scrapbook in one paw —and a plate of Christmas pudding in the other!'

'I don't care what he looks like,' said Mrs Brown, 'so long as he stays that way. The place wouldn't be the same without him.'

But Paddington was too far away to hear what was being said. He was already sitting up in bed, busily writing in his scrapbook.

First of all, there was a very important notice to go on the front page. It said:

PADINGTUN BROWN,

32 WINDSOR GARDENS,

LUNDUN,

ENGLAND,

YUROPE,

THE WORLD.

Then, on the next page he added, in large capital letters:
MY ADDVENTURES.   CHAPTER WUN.

Paddington sucked his pen thoughtfully for a moment and then carefully replaced the top on the bottle of ink before it had a chance to fall over on the sheets. He felt much too sleepy to write any more. But he didn't really mind. Tomorrow was another day—and he felt quite sure he *would* have some more adventures—even if he didn't know what they were going to be as yet.

Paddington lay back and pulled the blankets up round his whiskers. It was warm and comfortable and he sighed contentedly as he closed his eyes. It was nice being a bear. Especially a bear called Paddington.

from *More About Paddington*

The Frozen Bird
Anonymous

See, see, what a sweet little prize I have found!
A robin that lies half benumbed on the ground.
Well housed and well fed, in your cage you will sing,
And make our dull winter as gay as the spring.
But stay—sure 'tis cruel, with wings made to soar,
To be shut up in prison, and never fly more;
And I, who so often have longed for a flight,
To keep you a prisoner—would that be right?
No, come, pretty robin, I must set you free,
For your whistle, though sweet, would sound sadly to me.

The Red Robin
John Clare

Cock Robin, he got a new tippet in spring,
And he sat in a shed, and heard other birds sing.
And he whistled a ballad as loud as he could,
And built him a nest of oak leaves by the wood,
And finished it just as the celandine pressed
Like a bright burning blaze, by the edge of its nest,
All glittering with sunshine and beautiful rays,

Like high polished brass, or the fire in a blaze;
Then sung a new song on the edge of the brere;
And so it kept singing the whole of the year.
Till cowslips and wild roses blossomed and died,
The red robin sang by the old spinney side.

Memories of Christmas
Dylan Thomas

One Christmas was so much like another, in those years, around the sea town corner now, and out of all sound except the distant speaking of the voices I sometimes hear a moment before sleep, that I can never remember whether it snowed for six days and six nights when I was twelve or whether it snowed for twelve days and twelve nights when I was six; or whether the ice broke and the skating grocer vanished like a snowman through a white trap-door on that same Christmas Day that the mince-pies finished Uncle Arnold and we tobogganed down the seaward hill, all the afternoon, on the best tea-tray, and Mrs Griffiths complained, and we threw a snowball at her niece, and my hands burned so, with the heat and the cold, when I held them in front of the fire, that I cried for twenty minutes and then had some jelly.

All the Christmases roll down the hill towards the Welsh-speaking sea like a snowball growing whiter and bigger and rounder, like a cold and headlong moon bundling down the sky that was our street; and they stop at the rim of the ice-edged, fish-freezing waves, and I plunge my hands in the snow and bring out whatever I can find; holly or robins or pudding, squabbles and carols and oranges and tin whistles, and the

fire in the front room, and bang go the crackers, and holy, holy, holy, ring the bells, and the glass bells shaking on the tree, and Mother Goose, and Struwelpeter—oh! the baby-burning flames and the clacking scissorman!—Billy Bunter and Black Beauty, Little Women and boys who have three helpings, Alice and Mrs Potter's badgers, penknives, teddy-bears—named after a Mr Theodore Bear, their inventor, or father, who died recently in the United States—mouth-organs, tin-soldiers, and blancmange, and Auntie Bessie playing 'Pop Goes the Weasel' and 'Nuts in May' and 'Oranges and Lemons' on the untuned piano in the parlour all through the thimble-hiding musical-chairing blind-man's-buffing party at the end of the never-to-be-forgotten day at the end of the unremembered year.

In goes my hand into that wool-white bell-tongued ball of holidays resting at the margin of the carol-singing sea, and out come Mrs Prothero and the firemen.

It was on the afternoon of the day of Christmas Eve, and I was in Mrs Prothero's garden, waiting for cats, with her son Jim. It was snowing. It was always snowing at Christmas; December, in my memory, is white as Lapland, though there were no reindeers. But there were cats. Patient, cold, and callous, our hands wrapped in socks, we waited to snowball the cats. Sleek and long as jaguars and terrible-whiskered, spitting and snarling they would slink and sidle over the white back-garden walls, and the lynx-eyed hunters, Jim and I, fur-capped and moccasined trappers from Hudson's Bay off Eversley Road, would hurl our deadly snowballs at the green of their eyes. The wise cats never appeared. We were so still, Eskimo-footed arctic marksmen in the muffling silence of the eternal snows—eternal, ever since Wednesday—that we never heard Mrs Prothero's first cry from her igloo at the bottom of the garden. Or, if we heard it at all, it was, to us, like the far-off challenge of our enemy and prey, the neighbour's Polar Cat. But soon the voice grew louder. 'Fire!' cried Mrs Prothero, and she beat the dinner-gong. And we ran down the garden, with the snowballs in our arms, towards the house, and smoke, indeed, was pouring out of the dining-room, and the gong was bombilating, and Mrs Prothero was announcing ruin like a town-crier in Pompeii. This was better than all the cats in Wales standing on the wall in a row. We bounded into the house, laden with snowballs, and stopped at the open door of the smoke-filled room. Something was burning all right; perhaps it was Mr Prothero, who always slept there after mid-day dinner with a newspaper over his face; but he was standing in the middle of the room, saying 'A fine Christmas!' and smacking at the smoke with a slipper.

'Call the fire-brigade,' cried Mrs Prothero as she beat the gong.

'They won't be there,' said Mr Prothero, 'it's Christmas.'

There was no fire to be seen, only clouds of smoke and Mr Prothero standing in the middle of them, waving his slipper as though he were conducting.

'Do something,' he said.

And we threw all our snowballs into the smoke—I think we missed Mr Prothero—and ran out of the house to the telephone-box.

'Let's call the police as well,' Jim said.

'And the ambulance.'

'And Ernie Jenkins, he likes fires.'

But we only called the fire-brigade, and soon the fire-engine came and three tall men in helmets brought a hose into the house and Mr Prothero got out just in time before they turned it on. Nobody could have had a noisier Christmas Eve. And when the firemen turned off the hose and were standing in the wet and smoky room, Jim's aunt, Miss Prothero, came downstairs and peered in at them. Jim and I waited, very quietly, to hear what she would say to them. She said the right thing, always. She looked at the three tall firemen in their shining helmets, standing among the smoke and cinders and dissolving snowballs, and she said: 'Would you like something to read?'

Now out of that bright white snowball of Christmas gone comes the stocking, the stocking of stockings, that hung at the foot of the bed with the arm of a golliwog dangling over the top and small bells ringing in the toes. There was a company, gallant and scarlet but never nice to taste though I always tried when very young, of belted and busbied and musketed lead soldiers so soon to lose their heads and legs in the wars on the kitchen table after the tea-things, the mince-pies, and the cakes that I helped to make by stoning the raisins and eating them, had been cleared away; and a bag of moist and many-coloured jelly-babies and a folded flag and a false nose and a tram-conductor's cap and a machine that punched tickets and rang a bell; never a catapult; once, by a mistake that no one could explain, a little hatchet; and a rubber buffalo, or it may have been a horse, with a yellow head and haphazard legs; and a celluloid duck that made, when you pressed it, a most unducklike noise, a mewing moo that an ambitious cat might make who wishes to be a cow; and a painting-book in which I could make the grass, the trees, the sea, and the animals any colour I pleased: and still the dazzling sky-blue sheep are grazing in the red field under a flight of rainbow-beaked and pea-green birds.

Christmas morning was always over before you could say Jack Frost. And look! suddenly the pudding was burning! Bang the gong and call the fire-brigade and the book-loving firemen! Someone found the silver three-penny-bit with a currant on it; and the someone was always Uncle Arnold. The motto in my cracker read:

Let's all have fun this Christmas Day,
Let's play and sing and shout hooray!

and the grown-ups turned their eyes towards the ceiling, and Auntie Bessie, who had already been frightened, twice, by a clockwork mouse, whimpered at the sideboard and had some elderberry wine. And someone put a glass bowl full of nuts on

172

the littered table, and my uncle said, as he said once every year: 'I've got a shoe-nut here. Fetch me a shoe-horn to open it, boy.'

And dinner was ended.

And I remember that on the afternoon of Christmas Day, when the others sat around the fire and told each other that this was nothing, no, nothing, to the great snowbound and turkey-proud yule-log-crackling holly-berry-bedizined and kissing-under-the-mistletoe Christmas when *they* were children, I would go out, school-capped and gloved and muffled, with my bright new boots squeaking, into the white world on to the seaward hill, to call on Jim and Dan and Jack and to walk with them through the silent snowscape of our town.

We went padding through the streets, leaving huge deep footprints in the snow, on the hidden pavements.

'I bet people'll think there's been hippoes.'

'What would you do if you saw a hippo coming down Terrace Road?'

'I'd go like this, bang! I'd throw him over the railings and roll him down the hill and then I'd tickle him under the ear and he'd wag his tail . . .'

'What would you do if you saw *two* hippoes . . .?'

Iron-flanked and bellowing he-hippoes clanked and blundered and battered through the scudding snow towards us as we passed by Mr Daniel's house.

'Let's post Mr Daniel a snowball through his letter-box.'

'Let's write things in the snow.'

'Let's write "Mr Daniel looks like a spaniel" all over his lawn.'

'Look,' Jack said, 'I'm eating snow-pie.'

'What's it taste like?'

'Like snow-pie,' Jack said.

Or we walked on the white shore.

'Can the fishes see it's snowing?'

'They think it's the sky falling down.'

The silent one-clouded heavens drifted on to the sea.

'All the old dogs have gone.'

Dogs of a hundred mingled makes yapped in the summer at the sea-rim and yelped at the trespassing mountains of the waves.

'I bet St Bernards would like it now.'

And we were snowblind travellers lost on the north hills, and the great dewlapped dogs, with brandy-flasks round their necks, ambled and shambled up to us, baying 'Excelsior'.

We returned home through the desolate poor sea-facing streets where only a few children fumbled with bare red fingers in the thick wheel-rutted snow and cat-called after us, their voices fading away, as we trudged uphill, into the cries of the dock-birds and the hooters of ships out in the white and whirling bay.

Bring out the tall tales now that we told by the fire as we roasted chestnuts and the gaslight bubbled low. Ghosts with their heads under their arms trailed their chains and said 'whooo' like owls in the long nights when I dared not look over my shoulder; wild beasts lurked in the cubby-hole under the stairs where the gas-meter ticked. 'Once upon a time,' Jim said, 'there were three boys, just like us, who got lost in the dark in the snow, near Bethesda Chapel, and this is what happened to them. . . .' It was the most dreadful happening I had ever heard.

And I remember that we went singing carols once, a night or two before Christmas Eve, when there wasn't the shaving of a moon to light the secret, white-flying streets. At the end of a long road was a drive that led to a large house, and we stumbled up the darkness of the drive that night, each one of us afraid, each one holding a stone in his hand in case, and all of us too brave to say a word. The wind made through the drive-trees noises as of old and unpleasant and maybe web-footed men wheezing in caves. We reached the black bulk of the house.

'What shall we give them?' Dan whispered.

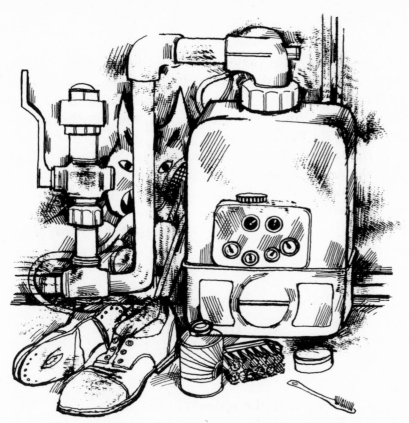

'"Hark the Herald"? "Christmas comes but Once a Year"?'
'No,' Jack said: 'We'll sing "Good King Wenceslas". I'll count three.'

One, two, three, and we began to sing, our voices high and seemingly distant in the snow-felted darkness round the house that was occupied by nobody we knew. We stood close together, near the dark door.

> Good King Wenceslas looked out
> On the Feast of Stephen.

And then a small, dry voice, like the voice of someone who has not spoken for a long time, suddenly joined our singing: a small, dry voice from the other side of the door: a small, dry voice through the keyhole. And when we stopped running we were outside *our* house; the front room was lovely and bright;

the gramophone was playing; we saw the red and white balloons hanging from the gas-bracket; uncles and aunts sat by the fire; I thought I smelt our supper being fried in the kitchen. Everything was good again, and Christmas shone through all the familiar town.

'Perhaps it was a ghost,' Jim said.

'Perhaps it was trolls,' Dan said, who was always reading.

'Let's go in and see if there's any jelly left,' Jack said. And we did that.

from *Quite Early One Morning*

Epiphany
Robert Herrick

Down with the rosemary, and so
Down with the bays and mistletoe;
Down with the holly, ivy, all
Wherewith ye dressed the Christmas hall;
That so the superstitious find
No one least branch there left behind;
For look, how many leaves there be
Neglected, there—maids, trust to me—
So many goblins you shall see.

Kindle the Christmas brand, and then
Till sunset let it burn;
Which quenched, then lay it up again
Till Christmas next return.
Parts must be kept wherewith to teend[1]

[1] Kindle.

The Christmas log next year,
And where 'tis safely kept, the fiend
Can do no mischief there.

End now the white loaf and the pie,
And let all sport with Christmas die.

Jenny Wren
Traditional

Jenny Wren fell sick;
   Upon a merry time,
In came Robin Redbreast,
   And brought her sops of wine.

'Eat well of the sop, Jenny,
   Drink well of the wine.'
'Thank you, Robin, kindly,
   You shall be mine.'

Jenny she got well,
   And stood upon her feet,
And told Robin plainly
   She loved him not a bit.

Robin, being angry,
   Hopp'd on a twig:
'Out upon you, fie upon you,
   Bold-faced jig!'

177

Mr Pickwick on the Ice
Charles Dickens

'Now,' said Wardle, after a substantial lunch, with the agreeable items of strong-beer and cherry-brandy, had been done ample justice to, 'what say you to an hour on the ice? We shall have plenty of time.'

'Capital!' said Mr Benjamin Allen.

'Prime!' ejaculated Mr Bob Sawyer.

'You skate, of course, Winkle?' said Wardle.

'Ye-yes, oh yes,' replied Mr Winkle. 'I—I—am *rather* out of practice.'

'Oh, *do* skate, Mr Winkle,' said Arabella. 'I like to see it so much.'

'Oh, it is *so* graceful,' said another young lady.

A third young lady said it was elegant, and a fourth expressed her opinion that it was 'swan-like'.

'I should be very happy, I'm sure,' said Mr Winkle, reddening; 'but I have no skates.'

This objection was at once overruled. Trundle had a couple of pair, and the fat boy announced that there were half a dozen more downstairs; whereat Mr Winkle expressed exquisite delight, and looked exquisitely uncomfortable.

Old Wardle led the way to a pretty large sheet of ice; and the fat boy and Mr Weller having shovelled and swept away the snow which had fallen on it during the night, Mr Bob Sawyer adjusted his skates with a dexterity which to Mr Winkle was perfectly marvellous, and prescribed circles with his left leg, and cut figures of eight, and inscribed upon the ice, without once stopping for breath, a great many other pleasant and astonishing devices, to the excessive satisfaction of Mr Pickwick, Mr Tupman, and the ladies; which reached a pitch of positive enthusiasm when old Wardle and Benjamin Allen, assisted by the aforesaid Bob Sawyer, performed some mystic evolutions which they called a reel.

All this time Mr Winkle, with his face and hands blue with the cold, had been forcing a gimlet into the soles of his feet, and putting his skates on with the points behind, and getting the straps into a very complicated and entangled state, with the assistance of Mr Snodgrass, who knew rather less about skates than a Hindoo. At length, however, with the assistance of Mr Weller, the unfortunate skates were firmly screwed and buckled on, and Mr Winkle was raised to his feet.

'Now, then, sir,' said Sam, in an encouraging tone; 'off vith you, and show 'em how to do it.'

'Stop, Sam, stop!' said Mr Winkle, trembling violently, and clutching hold of Sam's arms with the grasp of a drowning man. 'How slippery it is, Sam!'

'Not an uncommon thing upon ice, sir,' replied Mr Weller. 'Hold up, sir!'

This last observation of Mr Weller's bore reference to a demonstration Mr Winkle made, at the instant, of a frantic desire to throw his feet in the air and dash the back of his head on the ice.

'These—these—are very awkward skates; ain't they, Sam?' inquired Mr Winkle, staggering.

'I'm afeerd there's a orkard gen'l'm'n in 'em, sir,' replied Sam.

'Now, Winkle,' cried Mr Pickwick, quite unconscious that there was anything the matter. 'Come; the ladies are all anxiety.'

'Yes, yes,' replied Mr Winkle, with a ghastly smile; 'I'm coming.'

'Just a-goin' to begin,' said Sam, endeavouring to disengage himself. 'Now, sir, start off!'

'Stop an instant, Sam,' gasped Mr Winkle, clinging most affectionately to Mr Weller. 'I find I've got a couple of coats at home that I don't want, Sam. You may have them, Sam.'

'Thank'ee, sir,' replied Mr Weller.

'Never mind touching your hat, Sam,' said Mr Winkle, hastily; 'you needn't take your hand away to do that. I meant to have given you five shillings this morning for a Christmas box, Sam. I'll give it you this afternoon, Sam.'

'You're wery good, sir,' replied Mr Weller.

'Just hold me at first, Sam; will you?' said Mr Winkle. 'There—that's right. I shall soon get in the way of it, Sam. Not too fast, Sam; not too fast.'

Mr Winkle, stooping forward with his body half doubled up, was being assisted over the ice by Mr Weller, in a very singular and unswanlike manner, when Mr Pickwick most innocently shouted from the opposite bank:

'Sam!'

'Sir?' said Mr Weller.

'Here. I want you.'

'Let go, sir,' said Sam. 'Don't you hear the governor a-callin'? Let go, sir.'

With a violent effort, Mr Weller disengaged himself from the grasp of the agonized Pickwickian, and in so doing administered a considerable impetus to the unhappy Mr Winkle. With an accuracy which no degree of dexterity or practice could have ensured, that unfortunate gentleman bore swiftly down into the centre of the reel, at the very moment when Mr Bob Sawyer was performing a flourish of unparalleled beauty. Mr Winkle struck wildly against him, and with a loud crash they both fell heavily down. Mr Pickwick ran to the spot. Bob Sawyer had risen to his feet, but Mr Winkle was far too wise to do anything of the kind in skates. He was seated on the ice, making spasmodic efforts to smile; but anguish was depicted on every lineament of his countenance.

'Are you hurt?' inquired Mr Benjamin Allen, with great anxiety.

'Not much,' said Mr Winkle, rubbing his back very hard.

'I wish you'd let me bleed you,' said Mr Benjamin, with great eagerness.

'No, thank you,' replied Mr Winkle, hurriedly.

'I really think you had better,' said Allen.

'Thank you,' replied Mr Winkle, 'I'd rather not.'

'What do *you* think, Mr Pickwick?' inquired Bob Sawyer.

Mr Pickwick was excited and indignant. He beckoned to Mr Weller and said, in a stern voice, 'Take his skates off.'

'No; but really I had scarcely begun,' remonstrated Mr Winkle.

'Take his skates off,' repeated Mr Pickwick, firmly.

The command was not to be resisted. Mr Winkle allowed Sam to obey in silence.

'Lift him up,' said Mr Pickwick. Sam assisted him to rise.

Mr Pickwick retired a few paces apart from the bystanders, and beckoning his friend to approach, fixed a searching look upon him, and uttered, in a low but distinct and emphatic tone, these remarkable words:

'You're a humbug, sir.'

'A what?' said Mr Winkle, starting.

'A humbug, sir. I will speak plainer, if you wish it. An impostor, sir.'

With these words Mr Pickwick turned slowly on his heel, and rejoined his friends.

While Mr Pickwick was delivering himself of the sentiment just recorded, Mr Weller and the fat boy, having by their joint endeavours cut out a slide, were exercising themselves thereupon in a very masterly and brilliant manner. Sam Weller, in particular, was displaying that beautiful feat of fancy sliding which is currently denominated 'knocking at the cobbler's door', and which is achieved by skimming over the ice on one foot, and occasionally giving a twopenny postman's knock upon it with the other. It was a good long slide, and there was something in the motion which Mr Pickwick, who was very cold with standing still, could not help envying.

'It looks nice, warm exercise that, doesn't it?' he inquired of Wardle, when that gentleman was thoroughly out of breath by reason of the indefatigable manner in which he had converted his legs into a pair of compasses, and drawn complicated problems on the ice.

'Ah, it does indeed,' replied Wardle. 'Do you slide?'

'I used to do so, on the gutters, when I was a boy,' replied Mr Pickwick.

'Try it now,' said Wardle.

'Oh, do, please, Mr Pickwick!' cried all the ladies.

'I should be very happy to afford you any amusement,' replied Mr Pickwick, 'but I haven't done such a thing these thirty years.'

'Pooh! pooh! Nonsense!' said Wardle, dragging off his skates with the impetuosity which characterized all his proceedings. 'Here; I'll keep you company. Come along!' And away went the good-tempered old fellow down the slide, with a rapidity which came very close upon Mr Weller, and beat the fat boy all to nothing.

Mr Pickwick paused, considered, pulled off his gloves and put them in his hat; took two or three short runs, balked himself as often, and at last took another run, and went slowly and gravely down the slide, with his feet about a yard and a quarter apart, amidst the gratified shouts of all the spectators.

'Keep the pot a-bilin', sir!' said Sam; and down went Wardle again, and then Mr Pickwick, and then Sam, and then Mr Winkle, and then Mr Bob Sawyer, and then the fat boy, and then Mr Snodgrass, following closely upon each other's heels, and running after each other with as much eagerness as if all their future prospects in life depended on their expedition.

It was the most intensely interesting thing to observe the manner in which Mr Pickwick performed his share in the ceremony; to watch the torture of anxiety with which he viewed the person behind, gaining upon him at the imminent hazard of tripping him up; to see him gradually expend the painful force which he had put on at first, and turn slowly round on the slide, with his face towards the point from which he had started; to contemplate the playful smile which mantled on his face when he had accomplished the distance, and the eagerness with which he turned round when he had done so and ran after his predecessor—his black gaiters tripping pleasantly through the snow, and his eyes beaming cheerfulness and gladness through his spectacles. And when he was knocked down (which happened upon the average every third round), it was the most invigorating sight that can possibly be imagined to behold him gather up his hat, gloves, and handkerchief, with a glowing countenance, and resume his station in the rank with an ardour and enthusiasm that nothing could abate.

The sport was at its height, the sliding was at the quickest, the laughter was at the loudest, when a sharp, smart crack was heard. There was a quick rush towards the bank, a wild scream from the ladies, and a shout from Mr Tupman. A large mass of ice disappeared; the water bubbled up over it; Mr Pickwick's hat, gloves, and handkerchief were floating on the surface; and this was all of Mr Pickwick that anybody could see.

Dismay and anguish were depicted on every countenance; the males turned pale, and the females fainted; Mr Snodgrass and Mr Winkle grasped each other by the hand, and gazed at the spot where their leader had gone down, with frenzied eagerness; while Mr Tupman, by way of rendering the promptest assistance, and at the same time conveying to any persons who might be within hearing the clearest possible notion of the catastrophe, ran off across the country at his utmost speed, screaming 'Fire!' with all his might.

It was at this very moment, when old Wardle and Sam
Weller were approaching the hole with cautious steps, and Mr
Benjamin Allen was holding a hurried consultation with Mr
Bob Sawyer on the advisability of bleeding the company
generally, as an improving little bit of professional practice—
it was at this very moment that a face, head, and shoulders
emerged from beneath the water, and disclosed the features
and spectacles of Mr Pickwick.

'Keep yourself up for an instant—for only one instant!'
bawled Mr Snodgrass.

'Yes, do; let me implore you—for my sake!' roared Mr
Winkle, deeply affected. The adjuration was rather un-
necessary—the probability being that if Mr Pickwick had
declined to keep himself up for anybody else's sake, it would
have occurred to him that he might as well do so for his own.

'Do you feel the bottom there, old fellow?' said Wardle.

'Yes, certainly,' replied Mr Pickwick, wringing the water from his head and face, and gasping for breath. 'I fell upon my back. I couldn't get on my feet at first.'

The clay upon so much of Mr Pickwick's coat as was yet visible bore testimony to the accuracy of this statement; and as the fears of the spectators were still further relieved by the fat boy's suddenly recollecting that the water was nowhere more than five feet deep, prodigies of valour were performed to get him out. After a vast quantity of splashing, and cracking, and struggling, Mr Pickwick was at length fairly extricated from his unpleasant position, and once more stood on dry land.

'Oh, he'll catch his death of cold,' said Emily.

'Dear old thing!' said Arabella. 'Let me wrap this shawl round you, Mr Pickwick.'

'Ah, that's the best thing you can do,' said Wardle; 'and when you've got it on, run home as fast as your legs can carry you, and jump into bed directly.'

A dozen shawls were offered on the instant. Three or four of the thickest having been selected, Mr Pickwick was wrapped up, and started off, under the guidance of Mr Weller— presenting the singular phenomenon of an elderly gentleman, dripping wet, and without a hat, with his arms bound down to his sides, skimming over the ground, without any clearly-defined purpose, at the rate of six good English miles an hour.

But Mr Pickwick cared not for appearances in such an extreme case, and urged on by Sam Weller, he kept at the very top of his speed until he reached the door of Manor Farm, where Mr Tupman had arrived some five minutes before, and had frightened the old lady into palpitations of the heart by impressing her with the unalterable conviction that the kitchen chimney was on fire—a calamity which always presented itself in glowing colours to the old lady's mind when anybody about her evinced the smallest agitation.

Mr Pickwick paused not an instant until he was snug in bed.

from *The Pickwick Papers*

St George and the Dragon
A Traditional Cornish Christmas Play

Characters

SAINT GEORGE   KING OF EGYPT

THE DRAGON   TURKISH KNIGHT

FATHER CHRISTMAS   THE GIANT TURPIN

THE DOCTOR

Enter the TURKISH KNIGHT

Open your doors, and let me in,
I hope your favours I shall win;
Whether I rise or whether I fall,
I'll do my best to please you all.
St George is here, and swears he will come in,
And if he does, I know he'll pierce my skin.
If you will not believe what I do say,
Let Father Christmas come in—clear the way. [*Retires.*]

Enter FATHER CHRISTMAS
Here come I, old Father Christmas,
Welcome, or welcome not,
I hope old Father Christmas
Will never be forgot.

I am not come here to laugh or to jeer,
But for a pocketfull of money, and a skinfull of beer,
If you will not believe what I do say,
Come in, the King of Egypt!—clear the way!

Enter the KING OF EGYPT
Here I, the King of Egypt, boldly do appear,
St George, St George, walk in, my only son and heir.
Walk in, my son St George, and boldly act thy part,
That all the people here may see thy wond'rous art.

Enter SAINT GEORGE
Here come I, St George, from Britain did I spring,
I'll fight the Dragon bold, my wonders to begin.
I'll clip his wings, he shall not fly;
I'll cut him down, or else I die.

Enter THE DRAGON
Who's he that seeks the Dragon's blood,
And calls so angry, and so loud?
That English dog, will he before me stand?
I'll cut him down with my courageous hand.
With my long teeth, and scurvy jaw,
Of such I'd break up half a score,
And stay my stomach, till I'd more.
SAINT GEORGE *and* THE DRAGON *fight, the latter is killed.*
FATHER CHRISTMAS. Is there a doctor to be found
All ready, near at hand,
To cure a deep and deadly wound,
And make the champion stand.

Enter DOCTOR

Oh! yes, there is a doctor to be found
All ready, near at hand,
To cure a deep and deadly wound,
And make the champion stand.

FATHER CHRISTMAS. What can you cure?
DOCTOR. All sorts of diseases,
Whatever you pleases,
The phthisic, the palsy, and the gout;
If the devil's in, I'll blow him out.
FATHER CHRISTMAS. What is your fee?
DOCTOR. Fifteen pound, it is my fee,
The money to lay down.
But, as 'tis such a rogue as thee,
I cure for ten pound.

I carry a little bottle of alicumpane;
Here Jack, take a little of my flip flop,
Pour it down thy tip top;
Rise up and fight again.

THE DOCTOR *performs his cure, the fight is renewed, and* THE
DRAGON *again killed.*
SAINT GEORGE. Here am I, St George,
That worthy champion bold,
And with my sword and spear
I won three crowns of gold.
I fought the fiery dragon,
And brought him to the slaughter;
By that I won fair Sabra,
The King of Egypt's daughter.
Where is the man, that now will me defy?
I'll cut his giblets full of holes, and make his buttons fly.
The TURKISH KNIGHT *advances.*
Here come I, the Turkish Knight,
Come from the Turkish land to fight.

I'll fight St George, who is my foe,
I'll make him yield before I go;
He brags to such a high degree,
He thinks there's none can do the like of he.

SAINT GEORGE. Where is the Turk, that will before me stand?
I'll cut him down with my courageous hand.

They fight, the KNIGHT *is overcome, and falls on one knee.*

TURKISH KNIGHT. Oh! pardon me, St George, pardon of thee
I crave,
Oh! pardon me this night, and I will be thy slave.

SAINT GEORGE. No pardon shalt thou have, while I have foot
to stand,
So rise thee up again, and fight out sword in hand.

They fight again, and the KNIGHT *is killed.* FATHER CHRISTMAS
calls for THE DOCTOR, *with whom the same dialogue occurs as
before, and the cure is performed.*

Enter THE GIANT TURPIN.

Here come I, the Giant, bold Turpin is my name,
And all the nations round do tremble at my fame.
Where'er I go, they tremble at my sight,
No lord or champion long with me would fight.

SAINT GEORGE. Here's one that dares to look thee in the face,

189

And soon will send thee to another place.

They fight, and THE GIANT *is killed; medical aid is called in as before, and the cure performed by* THE DOCTOR, *to whom then is given a basin of girdy grout and a kick, and driven out.*

FATHER CHRISTMAS. Now, ladies and gentlemen, your sport
    is most ended,
    So prepare for the hat, which is highly commended.
    The hat it would speak, if it had but a tongue;
    Come throw in your money, and think it no wrong.

BOLD:

**TYPICALLY DESCRIBES ONE WHO IS
WILLING TO TAKE RISKS; WHO IS BRAVE
IN HEART AS WELL AS DEED**

BOLD TALES OF
BRAVE-HEARTED BOYS

SUSANNAH McFARLANE

ALADDIN
NEW YORK LONDON TORONTO SYDNEY NEW DELHI

ALADDIN

An imprint of Simon & Schuster Children's Publishing Division

1230 Avenue of the Americas, New York, New York 10020

First Aladdin hardcover edition October 2020

Text copyright © 2019 by Susannah McFarlane

Jacket illustrations copyright 2020: giant © Brenton McKenna; Hansel, Gretel, and witch © Simon Howe; thinking boy © Matt Huynh; dragons © Louie Joyce; birds © In Art & Bildagentur Zoonar GmbH/Shutterstock; additional images © Sandra Nobes/Allen & Unwin

Illustrations on pages 1-28 copyright © 2019 by Brenton McKenna

Illustrations on pages 29-58, pv & pvii copyright © 2019 by Simon Howe

Illustrations on pages 59-88 & pi copyright © 2019 by Matt Huynh

Illustrations on pages 89-118 & piii (dragon), pvi & p120 copyright © 2019 by Louie Joyce

Originally published in Australia in 2019 by Allen & Unwin as *Bold Tales for Brave-hearted Boys*

All rights reserved, including the right of reproduction in whole or in part in any form.

ALADDIN and related logo are registered trademarks of Simon & Schuster, Inc.

For information about special discounts for bulk purchases, please contact Simon & Schuster Special Sales at 1-866-506-1949 or business@simonandschuster.com.

The Simon & Schuster Speakers Bureau can bring authors to your live event.

For more information or to book an event contact the Simon & Schuster Speakers Bureau at 1-866-248-3049 or visit our website at www.simonspeakers.com.

Jacket designed by Sandra Nobes and Karin Paprocki

Interior designed by Sandra Nobes and Michael Rosamilia

The text of this book was set in Horley Old Style.

Manufactured in the United States of America 0720 FFG

2 4 6 8 10 9 7 5 3 1

Library of Congress Cataloging-in-Publication Data

Names: McFarlane, Susannah, author. | McKenna, Brenton, illustrator. | Howe, Simon, illustrator. | Huynh, Matt, illustrator. | Joyce, Louie, illustrator.

Title: Bold tales of brave-hearted boys / Susannah McFarlane ; Brenton McKenna, Simon Howe, Matt Huynh, Louie Joyce.

Description: First Aladdin hardcover edition. | New York : Aladdin, 2020. | Originally published: Crows Nest, Australia : Allen & Unwin, 2018. | Audience: Ages 5-9. | Summary: Reimagines four classic fairy tales with a twist to value kindness and honesty as much as strength and valor.

Identifiers: LCCN 2020019068 (print) | LCCN 2020019069 (ebook) | ISBN 9781534473591 (hardcover) | ISBN 9781534473607 (ebook)

Subjects: CYAC: Fairy tales. | Conduct of life—Fiction.

Classification: LCC PZ8 .M45787 Bol 2020 (print) | LCC PZ8 .M45787 (ebook) | DDC [Fic]—dc23

LC record available at https://lccn.loc.gov/2020019068

CONTENTS

For Edvard, the bravest,
most bold-hearted boy I know,
with love and admiration

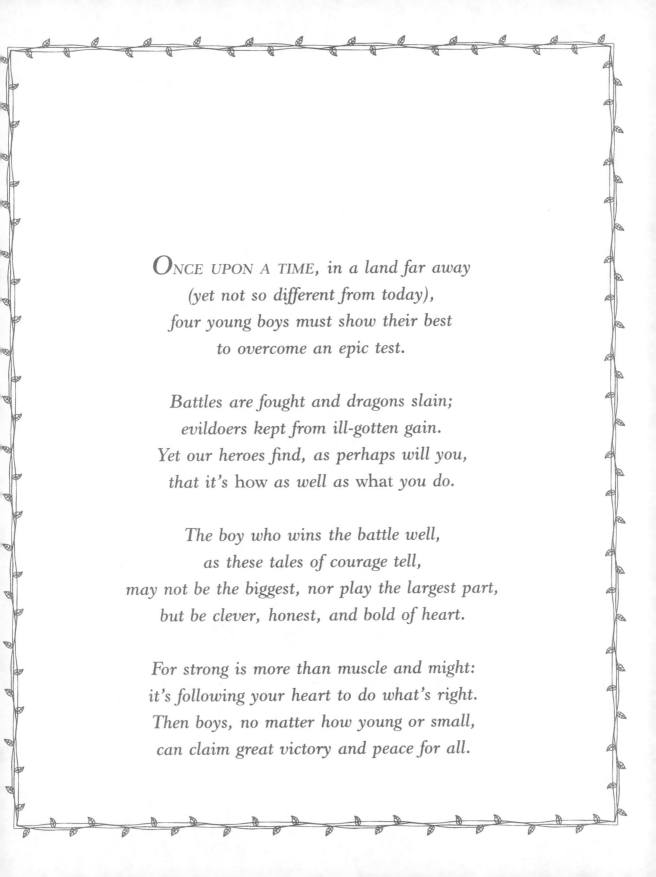

*O*NCE UPON A TIME, *in a land far away*
(yet not so different from today),
four young boys must show their best
to overcome an epic test.

Battles are fought and dragons slain;
evildoers kept from ill-gotten gain.
Yet our heroes find, as perhaps will you,
that it's how as well as what you do.

The boy who wins the battle well,
as these tales of courage tell,
may not be the biggest, nor play the largest part,
but be clever, honest, and bold of heart.

For strong is more than muscle and might:
it's following your heart to do what's right.
Then boys, no matter how young or small,
can claim great victory and peace for all.

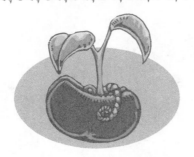

JACK AND THE BEANSTALK

1.

ONCE UPON A TIME in the Upper Lands, high in the sky, lived a boy called Jack. Jack was a good boy, gentle and helpful. Each morning, after taking tea and toast to his mother in bed, making sure the slices were spread with just the right amount of butter and jam, Jack would set off for the woods. There he'd uproot pine trees, to be made into furniture in a nearby village called the Tablelands. For Jack, or Gentle Jack, or GJ as his mother and pretty much everyone in the villages called him, was a giant, and pulling up the tall trees was the perfect job for him.

No one was sure why GJ was a giant, he just was—and, as it happened, his size was just what was needed for his special job. In fact, everyone in the Upper Lands had their own special job to do, needing their exact special talent.

Each time GJ pulled up a tree in the woods, he'd take a pine seed from his large pocket and plant it in the hole left behind. Everything grew quickly in the Upper Lands, nourished by the silver rain that fell from the sky, and in just weeks a new tree would be ready to be harvested. Despite having enormous fingers, GJ was very careful to place each tiny seed in exactly the right place, spreading just the right amount of dirt over it, grinning as the first green shoots popped up immediately.

GJ was happy in his work, and because he was also a creative boy, he liked making up little chants as he walked, pulled, and planted.

Hey, ho, hi, hum,
heave the trees, up they come!
Drop the seed, wait a mo',
see the tree begin to grow!

GJ stacked his trees against a huge boulder in a big clearing, one atop another. When he'd stacked fifty trees, it'd be time for his favorite part of the job: tree-snagging. GJ had developed his very own tree-snagging technique, lassoing the trees together with a long, long rope. Each time, he'd test himself by trying to

do this from farther away from the stack. Now GJ could snag the pile and haul it toward him from a mile away, an amazing record for even a boy of GJ's size.

GJ would then haul the wood to the Tablelands, where the villagers milled it and crafted it into beautiful tables and chairs.

"Great bundle today, big guy," called the mayor of the Tablelands one morning as GJ arrived.

"Thank you, sir," replied GJ, beaming. "Oh, and here's your egg." He took a gleaming golden egg from his shirt pocket and handed it to the mayor.

That was another
special thing about
GJ. On the day
he was born, a
white goose
walked into
his mother's
farmhouse. That

would have been strange enough, but even stranger was that
this goose laid golden eggs, one every day.

"It was a day of double blessing," GJ's mother always said.
"Precious eggs and an even more precious boy with a heart so big

it needed the body of
a giant to hold it!"

And so, each day,
when he delivered
the wood, Jack
also brought an
egg. A villager
would carry it
off to the smelter,
where it would be

melted down into gold coins and shared among all who lived in the Upper Lands.

"Thank you, GJ," said the mayor, "and here are some coins for you and your mother."

As he spoke, a team of villagers arrived with a very tall ladder. GJ knelt down and they leaned the ladder against him. Then one of the villagers climbed up and handed him a bulging cloth sack.

"There's a bit more today so you can buy materials for your project," she said. "And we've popped in one of your favorite candies. The sweet-maker spent all day spinning the sugar for you."

GJ's smile grew wider as he took out a huge red-and-yellow-striped whopper-sucker all-day lollipop.

"Thank you, everyone," he cried. "Delicious! And that's exactly how many coins I need to buy the metal for my Incredible Flower-Pulling Machine!"

"Our pleasure, GJ. You deserve it," said the mayor.

As he walked home, GJ sucked on his lollipop and thought about the metal he'd buy in the Ironlands the next day after he'd finished work. While GJ was the perfect boy for picking trees, picking the tiny, delicate flowers his mother liked in her tea was tricky for him. The contraption he'd designed would be just the thing for that.

That evening, over dinner, GJ told his mother about his day and his plans for the Incredible Flower-Pulling Machine. After stacking the plates in the dish-scrubbing box he'd invented, leaving the coins on the table ready for the following day, GJ helped his mother into bed, brought her a cup of tea, made sure she was comfortable, and leaned down, down, down to kiss her good night.

"You're a good son, GJ," she said, kissing the top of his giant nose. "And remember, when in doubt . . ."

"Do good," said GJ.

"Exactly," replied his mother. "Sleep well, my giant-hearted boy."

GJ smiled and tiptoed out, leaving her door slightly ajar so she'd hear the beautiful lullabies their magical golden harp, a gift from the villagers, would play for them throughout the night.

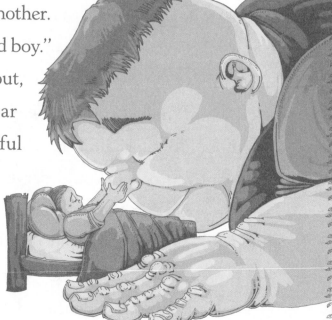

But that night, lying in his giant bed, GJ had to strain to hear his harp above the sounds of some angry voices floating up from the Lower Lands below him.

"Foolish boy, you gave our last cow to someone for five beans? *Beans?* What were you thinking?" snapped a woman's voice.

"But, Mother," a boy's voice cried, "the man said they were magic! And it would have taken so long to walk the cow all the way to the market."

"Lazy, disobedient boy!" replied the mother. "Magic? Honestly, Jack, how could you be so stupid?"

Another Jack? thought GJ. *He may have the same name as me, but my mother and I don't argue like that.*

Below in the Lower Lands, a door slammed and the voices finally quieted, so that GJ could hear the harp's soothing lullaby again.

"Thank goodness," he murmured as his eyelids started drooping. In seconds, the giant boy was asleep and all was peaceful and calm in the Upper Lands.

2.

THAT NIGHT, as everyone in
both lands slept, something
strange was happening in
the Lower Lands. Jack's
mother had thrown the
beans her son had brought
home out the kitchen door in
disgust, slamming it shut
after them. The beans
had landed in an unused
vegetable plot, and now
a beanstalk took root and
began to grow . . . fast.

It grew higher than the
weeds and thistles.

It grew higher than
the farmhouse and all
the surrounding trees.

In fact, it grew higher than everything in the Lower Lands, and by the next morning it had grown right up through the clouds into the Upper Lands.

But when GJ headed off to work the next morning, he knew none of this. He didn't see the beanstalk, nor the very small boy hauling himself up it, through the swirling, misty cloud mantle.

That small boy was the Lower Lands Jack, who now stood in the Upper Lands. In the distance, he could see a house.

Hmmm, worth a look, thought Jack. *You never know your luck.* As Jack got closer to the house, he realized it was tall—very tall. *A giant must live here,* he thought as he reached the door. *It would take at least twenty of me to even reach the keyhole! Maybe the giant has treasure!*

To Jack's surprise, the door was open. (For there was no need to lock doors in the Upper Lands.) He went inside and found himself in a kitchen with a fireplace, a very high table, one very large low chair, and one very small high chair.

Definitely a giant, decided Jack, climbing up a long coil of rope hanging from the high table. "My!" he cried as he stepped onto the table and spied the coins, which GJ had forgotten to take with him that morning. "Treasure! This is indeed my lucky day. And I deserve these coins. I'm sure whoever lives here doesn't need them half as much as I do. I might even give my mother some, if she's lucky."

"Is there someone out there?" came a thin voice from another room, making Jack jump with fright. It was GJ's mother.

Then, much to his surprise, music began to play. Jack spun around, knocking over a sugar bowl on the table, to see a golden harp by the fireplace playing music—alarmingly loud music, all by itself.

Next, the house began to shake. "This house is enchanted!" cried Jack, and he ran across the table, leaving little boot prints in the sugar. He snatched the coins and slid back down the rope to the kitchen floor.

The house was shaking because GJ was running toward it. He'd not gone far from home when his nose had begun to twitch—for Upper Landers had an exceptional sense of smell.

Fee, fi, fo, fum,
I smell the scent of a Lower Lands man.
I will rush so I can see
who this Lower Lander might be!

And so GJ had run toward the smell. It wasn't often that visitors made their way to the Upper Lands, and GJ was eager to learn how the stranger had got there. He was a little surprised, however, when he realized he was running in the direction of his own house. His surprise turned to fear when he heard his harp wailing, and he ran faster and harder, his steps now thundering on the ground.

Jack, meanwhile, looked longingly at the golden harp by the fireplace, but he knew he had no time to lose and he dashed out the door toward the beanstalk. By the time GJ reached home, Jack was back in the Lower Lands.

GJ rushed in the front door. He saw the overturned bowl and the tiny boot prints in the sugar on the table, and realized with consternation that the sacks of gold coins were gone. Whoever would take something that didn't belong to them? That simply didn't happen in the Upper Lands.

"GJ, is that you?" came his mother's voice.

"Mom!" he cried, rushing into her room. "Are you all right?"

GJ was so relieved his mother was unharmed that he burst into tears and all but forgot about the coins. His mom gave his cheek a big hug and wiped his tears away, which made GJ feel a lot better—but what on earth, they wondered, was going on?

3.

THE NEXT MORNING, GJ didn't want to leave his mother, but she insisted. "You must do your work, GJ," she said gently. "The Tablelands depend on you."

So GJ set off reluctantly, sad he no longer had the coins to buy iron for his machine, and worried about his mom.

> *Bish, bash, bo, bum,*
> *I am feeling a little glum . . .*

GJ chanted with less than his usual vigor as he walked the path to the woods. Once he reached the woods, however, and could breathe the fresh air and hear the chirping, buzzing, busy noises of the woodland animals, GJ quickly cheered up and set to work.

Meanwhile, down in the Lower Lands, Jack was setting off up the beanstalk again, a large empty sack on his back. He planned to steal the golden harp, for it would fetch a pretty penny at the markets. So off he went, through the cloud mantle again and into GJ's house.

Jack was relieved to hear snoring coming from the bedroom this time. He tiptoed toward the hearth where, as he'd hoped, he saw the harp—and, to his surprise, a goose sitting next to it.

"Hello, my pretty," he whispered. "I didn't notice you last time. You look good and plump; you'll make a nice Sunday dinner, for sure. I'll take you, too."

Jack picked up the goose only to jump back in surprise and delight: there beneath it was a large golden egg.

"Yes!" hissed Jack. "I'll never have to work again! The giant must have hundreds of eggs and doesn't need any more—and I most certainly do!" And he greedily stuffed the harp and the goose and the golden egg into his sack, the cloth muffling the noise of the harp.

"The sooner I melt you into gold the better," he said, tying up the sack. Then he threw it over his shoulder and ran out of the house toward the beanstalk.

In the forest, GJ got the twitching feeling in his nose again.

Fee, fi, fo, fum,
I smell the scent of that Lower Lands man.

GJ took off, running as fast as he could. This time, the scent led him to the very edge of the Upper Lands, where he saw the top tendrils of the beanstalk. Peering through the cloud mantle, he saw the enormous beanstalk twisting downward and could just make out a small boy far below.

GJ wasted no time. He leaped onto the beanstalk and clambered after the boy. With his long legs, he soon caught up. He plucked the boy from the stalk.

"Oi!" cried the boy. GJ dangled him in front of his face, studying him. "What are you doing?" yelled the boy crossly.

"What am I doing?" asked GJ. "What are *you* doing? You're Jack, aren't you?"

"What's it to you?" snapped the boy. "Put me down!"

Just then, a muffled *honk* came from the sack over Jack's back, followed by a frantic-sounding harp melody. Realizing that this boy surely had stolen his coins the day before, and was now bold enough to have stolen both his family's beautiful harp *and* their beloved goose, GJ began to feel very, very cross indeed. He pinched the boy

a little more tightly, and Jack realized he was in no position to make demands of this giant.

"I mean, I'm sorry, Mr. Giant," he said whiningly. "Please let me go."

"Did you take my coins yesterday?"

"No," said Jack, gulping.

GJ pulled Jack even closer toward him. He wanted to see his eyes more closely, for he wasn't at all sure he believed him. Jack, however, thought the giant was about to eat him, so he changed his story.

"Yes!" he cried. "I mean yes! I am sorry, truly! I only did it because we're so poor, and I wanted to help my old, sick—very, very sick—mother. I was doing it for her. Please don't hurt me. I'll never steal again, I promise. Please, kind sir, I beg you, don't eat me."

GJ was taken aback—he had no idea why Jack thought

he would eat him—but Jack's talk of helping his mother had made GJ feel less cross toward him. Perhaps Jack needed the coins more than he did. Perhaps this was his chance to do some good?

"Hmm," said GJ, not realizing that a giant *hmmm* can sound rather frightening if you aren't used to hearing it.

"Please!" shrieked Jack. "I'll do anything!"

"Okay," said GJ, plucking the sack from the boy's back. "I want my harp and my goose back, but you can keep the egg, for your mother."

"What?" said Jack. *Why would he do that?* he wondered.

"You heard me—keep the egg," said GJ, putting Jack back on a lower branch of the beanstalk. "But keep your promise, never steal again—and never come to the Upper Lands again either."

Jack scampered down the beanstalk without so much as a thank you to GJ. *I don't want that lump changing his mind about that golden egg and coming down after me,* he thought as he reached the ground. *I'll chop down the beanstalk.* And he grabbed the axe from the pile of unchopped wood in his yard and started hacking at the base of the stalk.

"Hey!" shouted GJ, who was still halfway up it. "Stop it, or the beanstalk will fall and I'll die!"

"Not my problem!" cried Jack, swinging the axe again and again. As the beanstalk wobbled, GJ dropped the sack with the harp and goose in it and it fell and caught on one of the beanstalk's lower shoots.

GJ had to get his goose back—the villagers would be lost without its eggs—but the beanstalk was getting wobblier and wobblier. GJ was scared. He didn't want to fall. He looked up: he could retreat home, where he'd be safe, but then what about the goose? GJ took a giant breath and started climbing downward instead.

Jack had also seen the sack drop, and now he raced up the beanstalk, greed overtaking him. "Stupid, clumsy giant," he cried, "I'll have my harp and goose after all."

Jack was nimbler than GJ, and he

reached the sack first, snatching it and beginning to climb back down. But GJ had an idea. He uncoiled his tree-snagging rope, looked directly at the sack, swung the rope down, and snagged the sack! Then he started climbing for home, the sack trailing after him.

"Hey!" shouted Jack. "You can't! It's mine!"

"No, it's not," called GJ over his shoulder.

Rage overtook Jack. As GJ hauled himself safely back to the Upper Lands, panting in relief, Jack began climbing after GJ up the now very wobbly beanstalk.

Then, from below, GJ heard a cry: "Help, help! I'm stuck and the beanstalk is about to fall!" It was coming from down the beanstalk. It was Jack.

GJ was horrified. *Jack will surely die*, he thought. *But if I try to help him, so might I. And he treated me really badly.*

"Help!"

GJ knew he couldn't stand by and let Jack die, no matter how badly he'd behaved—he had to do the right thing and help. He climbed back onto the beanstalk. The wind blew strongly, and the beanstalk swung terribly from side to side, but GJ carried on until he found Jack tangled in a broken beanstalk tendril.

Crack!

The beanstalk lurched to one side. *It's starting to fall!* GJ realized. He plucked up Jack, who fainted in shock. GJ put him in his pocket. Then he pushed on down the beanstalk, dropped the boy onto a soft haystack, and climbed back upward as fast as he could.

Crack!

The beanstalk lurched again. There were more cracks and groans as huge tendrils began to fall around him.

GJ pushed on and up. He was nearly there. If he could just—

Crack!

With that last crack Jack woke up, in time to see the beanstalk crash to earth.

Had the giant who'd saved his life made it back to the Upper Lands? Jack didn't know.

4.

ONE BRIGHT MORNING just a few days later, after making his mother toast and tea in bed, Jack was up early. He'd spent the past days cleaning away the beanstalk branches and tending to the vegetable garden. He'd decided he'd like to grow food for himself and his mother.

Jack was taking a break when, on the front step, he saw a small box attached to a parachute. He removed the strings and opened the box. Inside were three golden eggs.

A huge smile broke across Jack's face. This could only be from the giant. He'd made it back up to the Upper Lands—he was safe! He must have made that clever parachute, too.

Jack looked down again at the eggs, and as tears pricked his eyes, he felt something he hadn't felt before. "Why would he do that? For me, who stole from him?" he whispered aloud. "I don't deserve this." He looked up at the clear blue sky above. "Thank you," he said. "I'll do something really good with them. I promise."

And he did—and both Jacks and their families lived happily ever after.

HANSEL AND GRETEL

1.

ONCE UPON A TIME, in a land ravaged by failing crops and famine, lived twins called Hansel and Gretel. A spell had been cast over the land, hardening the ground and the hearts of those who tried to till it. Disease was rife, and the twins' parents were taken by illness, leaving them to the reluctant charity of their uncle and aunt, who lived in a small cottage on the edge of a large wood.

The aunt and uncle toiled hard each day. They chopped firewood to sell in the village, but no one had money to spare. Often the most they'd manage to exchange before the long walk home were a few stale buns and a bag of flour. At home, they'd mix the flour sparingly with water to make bread and, using the leaves of the few stunted cabbages that managed to grow, boil a watery soup. But none of it was ever enough to fill their stomachs, and the poor family groaned with hunger from morning until night.

"What will become of us?" wailed the aunt to her husband. "Soon winter will come, and we'll not even have these cabbages to eat. We can barely feed ourselves, let alone your poor dead brother's children. This can't go on!"

Hansel and Gretel tried to help. Gretel, who was strong and loved to be outside, helped chop wood while Hansel, who wasn't so strong but was exceptionally good at solving puzzles, ordered the logs in perfect piles outside the kitchen. Gretel stoked the fire with the heavy metal poker, while Hansel carefully measured out flour and water, using as little as possible to make the most bread.

But there was never enough food.

"How will we survive?" lamented the aunt, stirring the watery soup. "We'll surely starve!"

Each night Hansel and Gretel climbed up to their straw mattress in the attic. Lying side by side, they'd tell each other stories to take their minds off their rumbling stomachs.

Gretel made up stories of great adventure, in which she'd rescue someone— usually Hansel—from ravenous wolves in the woods, or eye-pecking birds that swooped down from the sky. Gretel's eyes always shone as she told these stories. Hansel would often interrupt to ask the details: How many wolves were there? How big were the ravens?

Other times, Hansel told
Gretel instead how one
day they'd have a little shop,
where they'd make and sell all manner
of delicious things that for now, huddled
in their straw bed, they could only dream of:
gingerbread cookies, candy-striped lollipops, and soft-centered
caramels that people would come from far and wide to buy.

Then the twins would snuggle into each other, and, their
breathing falling into the same rhythm, they'd sleep until their
hunger pains woke them the next morning.

One moon-bright autumn night Hansel and Gretel heard their uncle and aunt talking in hushed tones downstairs.

"This can't go on, I tell you," said the aunt. "We will all surely die!"

"The children are of little help," said the uncle, "yet they have hungry stomachs to fill."

The twins looked at each other sadly. Then the voices below became lower still, and they couldn't make out the words, until they heard their uncle say at last, "It's decided."

"It's the only way," agreed the aunt. "And, after all, they are not our children."

"Tomorrow, first thing," said the uncle, "I'll tell them we need to chop wood, take them deep into the forest, and leave them there."

Hansel and Gretel were horrified, for they'd heard of the witches and wolves that stalked the deep woods. No one dared go in, not even to find the sweet berries said to grow there.

"I'll stop this, Hansel!" whispered Gretel fiercely. "I'll go down and tell them—"

"No, sister," said Hansel, "we need a plan, to show them we can be useful."

"True, brother," replied Gretel. "But how?"

"If we go into the woods," replied Hansel, looking out the attic window to the moonlit yard below, "we can collect berries for us all to eat."

Gretel thought of the wolves, then squared her shoulders. "I can carry lots," she said. "But how will we get home?"

Hansel furrowed his brow, a sign he was thinking. He was looking at some white stones in the yard, gleaming in the moonlight.

"We'll make a trail to lead us back," he said, "with those white stones. We need to collect them now—but how do we get down there without Uncle and Aunt seeing?"

"Leave that to me," said Gretel with a glint in her eyes.

Gretel ran to the window and shimmied down the cottage wall. She stuffed stones into the large pockets of her grubby pinafore, climbed back up, and emptied the pile of stones onto their bed not three minutes later.

"You did it!" said Hansel.

"We did it," replied Gretel, grinning. They put their thumbs together in their secret handshake, and as they snuggled back into bed, Hansel told Gretel the rest of his plan.

2.

THE NEXT MORNING, as the cockerel crowed, the uncle called gruffly, "Come down, children. We have work to do in the woods."

Hansel and Gretel looked at each other, put their thumbs together, and nodded. Then Hansel filled his pockets with the white stones and they climbed down the ladder into the kitchen.

"Ready, Uncle," they said.

"Here," said the wife curtly. "A crust of bread each for the way."

The three set off into the woods in silence, chewing their crusts, trying to make each mouthful last as long as it could. Hansel dropped white stones at regular intervals.

Deep in the woods, the uncle stopped. "Wait here, children. I'll chop wood, then fetch you to help carry it."

"Yes, Uncle," replied Hansel and Gretel, but they knew he was lying. He walked away, looking back only once at the two children in the dark woods.

When he was gone, Hansel said, "Now for our plan, sister. We'll collect more berries in one day than we've had all autumn. When we return, Uncle and Aunt will be so happy they'll allow us to stay."

Indeed, there were many more ripe, juicy berries growing in these woods than at the cottage. Gretel, being faster and stronger, collected the most, but Hansel checked them all, making sure none were rotten.

As the day neared its end, their pockets bulged. Now they turned toward home, eyes on the ground, looking for the white stones.

Gretel ran ahead, calling back to her brother, "Here's one, Hansel! Here's another! Your plan worked—you did it!"

"We did it," replied her brother.

Gretel waited patiently as Hansel caught up with her before dashing ahead again . . . and it was nearly dark when they reached the cottage and burst through the kitchen door.

"Look, Uncle! Look, Aunt!" cried Gretel.

"We have berries!" cried Hansel.

But their aunt and uncle only stared at them and then each other, not even noticing the berries bulging in the children's pockets. Hansel and Gretel watched, crestfallen, as the adults whispered. Then the uncle said harshly to the children: "Did I not tell you to wait in the woods?"

"Yes, Uncle," said Gretel, "but—"

"Are the berries to make up for disobedience?" asked the aunt sharply.

"We'll return to the woods. Now," said the uncle. "You'll do as I say."

Hansel and Gretel were alarmed. There was no time to collect more stones. What would they do?

Hansel furrowed his brow. "We're sorry, Uncle, but may we have some more bread?" he asked.

"Ha!" said the uncle. "Always thinking of yourselves."

But the aunt's heart softened a little. "It will be the last you take, I suppose," she muttered to herself, sighing as she handed over two crusts. "Now go!"

Gretel went to eat the bread. "Don't eat it, Gretel," whispered Hansel. "I have a plan."

The children followed as their uncle led them back into the woods, taking a different path from last time. This time Hansel broke off crumbs of bread and dropped them along the way.

Gretel saw what her brother was doing. "Good plan, brother," she whispered. Hansel wasn't so sure.

It was dark when the uncle stopped. "Stay here," he said. "Do not disobey me again." This time he did not look back.

"Now what?" asked Gretel.

"We wait until morning," said Hansel. "Then we'll follow the crumbs back."

A wolf howled, and both children jumped.

"I'm a bit scared," said Hansel.

"So am I," said Gretel.

"But we have each other," said Hansel.

"Yes," said Gretel.

And the two children smiled, put their thumbs together, and nodded.

"Look, Hansel," cried Gretel, "I can gather up the fallen leaves to keep us warm."

While his sister scooped up the leaves, Hansel found a sheltered spot under a large oak tree. The twins snuggled into each other and ate their berries for dinner. Then, with their blanket of leaves offering some comfort from the cold night air, they fell asleep.

3.

THE CHILDREN WOKE to sunbeams pushing through the forest trees and ants crawling across their legs and arms.

Gretel leaped up, stamping her feet furiously. "That will only make them angry," advised Hansel softly. "Let's go home."

"Yes," cried Gretel, running ahead, searching for the crumbs. But she couldn't find a single one.

"None here, Hansel!" she cried, again and again. Finally she spotted one, but a black raven swooped down, screeching, and picked it up in its beak.

"Birds have eaten all the crumbs," said Hansel. "I should have thought of that. We're lost!"

"But we have each other," said Gretel.

"Yes," said Hansel, managing a little smile, "but we are still lost."

"I can choose the clearest path for us," said Gretel. "Come on, brother."

And so the children walked on deeper into the woods, Gretel thrashing at the undergrowth when it blocked their path, using a large stick she'd found. Hansel, meanwhile, pointed out the odd dangerous insect and poisonous plant they needed to avoid. Between them they managed to walk quite some way, avoiding the stinging nettles and biting ants of the wood. After some hours they came to a clearing. At its far end, they saw a cottage.

"Perhaps whoever lives there might give us something to eat," said Gretel, and ran ahead. When she got closer, she turned back. "Oh, quick, Hansel," she shouted. "Come quickly. You'll never believe this!"

Indeed, the cottage was no ordinary cottage. While it had a door with two windows on either side and a roof, as most cottages do, this cottage wasn't made of stone, nor wood nor thatching. Instead, it was made entirely of things one could eat—mouthwateringly sweet things Hansel and Gretel had never dreamt of seeing, let alone eating. The walls were made

of gingerbread, with pink-and-white icing piped up and down. Inlaid in the icing were marshmallows and hard candies—blue, yellow, red, and purple. Licorice lined the window frames, and the windowsills held tiny cupcakes with lashings of frosted icing in all the colors of the rainbow. Jelly-chews formed heart shapes on the shutters. A little fence of candy canes circled the cottage, and cotton-candy flowers on toffee stems stood in gingerbread flowerpots by the door.

To the side of the cottage was a vegetable patch, but sprouting from the soil of grated chocolate was even more candy: caramel popcorn grew in clusters on a honeycomb-trellised vine of peppermint jelly leaves; hard candies as big as pumpkins grew from sprawling green licorice roots;

strawberry sherbet bombs burst from white chocolate flowers; and heads of soft jelly-drops grew like broccoli on thick stalks of green marzipan. Next to the patch, lemon-drop and toffee-apple tree branches bent over from the abundance of candy-fruit on them.

Hansel and Gretel couldn't believe their eyes—or their noses. They licked their lips and gazed about in wonder.

"We have to try some, Gretel," said Hansel, carefully removing a candy cane from the path and giving it a huge lick. "Oh, it's delicious!"

Gretel took a cupcake from a windowsill and took a large bite. Jam oozed out of the cake, mingling deliciously in her mouth with the frosted icing. "Hansel!" she exclaimed. "Can this be real?"

But it was real, and soon the starving children were trying everything they could reach, filling their stomachs with candies and lollipops, caramel-filled chocolates and strawberry marsh-mallows.

There was a creak as the front door opened. An old, shaky-sounding voice came from inside. "Nibble, nibble, like a mouse. Is someone nibbling at my house?"

Hansel and Gretel jumped back, mouths full, as an old woman hobbled outside. She was dressed in a long black dress with a frilly white collar, and a red apron embroidered with little white hearts. She leaned heavily on a wooden cane.

Her face was lined with wrinkles, and her eyes were an odd red color, yet she looked kind. She had rosy cheeks and her hair was in a soft bun, tendrils swirling around her face like cotton candy. She smiled a friendly smile, but then squinted as she hobbled closer, her nose twitching.

"I can't see a thing," she said, "but I can smell lovely children." The closer she got to Hansel and Gretel, the more her nose twitched. "Ah, yes, how delightful—children! Come closer, my sweet lovelies. Let me feel you."

Hansel and Gretel didn't move.

"No need to fear," said the old woman. "Let's have a look at you." She'd reached them now, and she pinched their cheeks and arms. "You're a strong one, aren't you?" she said to Gretel. "Hmmm, too muscly. What about you, boy?" She pinched his thin arm again. "Not much fat on you, is there?"

"I've always been small," said Hansel, "and we hardly eat."

"Well, that's no good at all," replied the woman. "We need to fatten you up—otherwise you're no good to me, are you?"

Hansel wondered what she meant by that, but Gretel was already chewing on a caramel the old woman had pushed into her mouth. "Now, do come inside, my sweeties, and I'll make you each a large mug of hot chocolate with marshmallows."

Hansel and Gretel looked at each other and nodded. If the old woman had made such delicious sweets, surely she was kind. "Thank you!" they said, following her into the house.

As they entered, though, the door slammed shut behind them, and when the old woman turned back, her face had changed. Her mouth had twisted into a mean snarl, and her red eyes flashed.

"You, my dears, are good enough to eat," she said with a thin laugh, "or at least you, boy, will be once I fatten you up!"

The children realized the old woman was a witch and had used her magical house to lure them in, but it was too late to escape. The door was locked, and as the witch banged her cane three times on the floor an iron cage fell down, imprisoning Hansel. Gretel pulled at the cage bars.

"Stop it, girl! Save your strength for chopping my wood, stirring my batter, and feeding your brother."

"No!" cried Gretel, pulling harder at the bars.

"There's no escape," the witch said simply. "You'll do as I say. I may not be much for seeing, but I can smell you perfectly. One move I don't command and your brother will be baked."

Hansel and Gretel shook with fear. They were trapped.

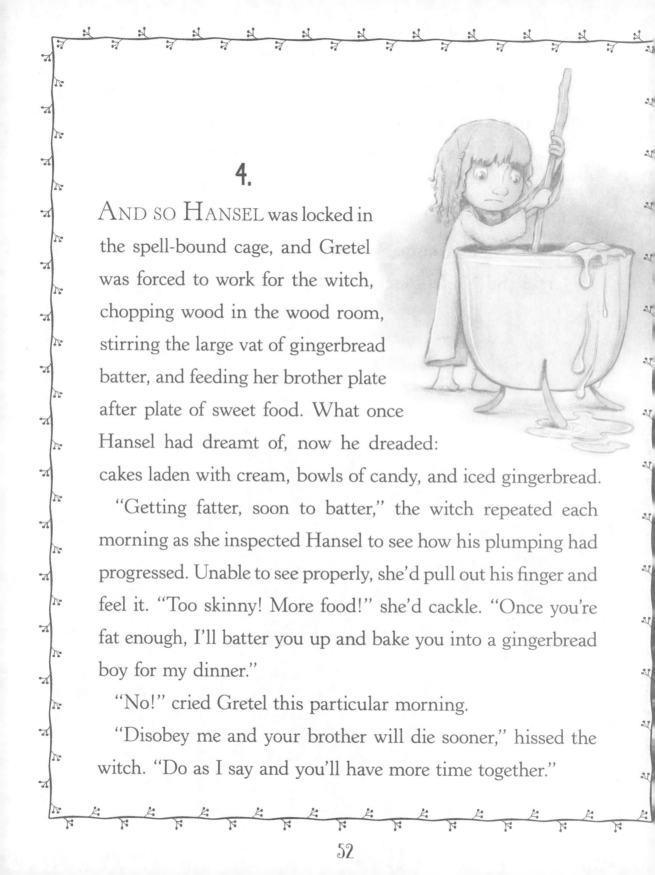

4.

AND SO HANSEL was locked in
the spell-bound cage, and Gretel
was forced to work for the witch,
chopping wood in the wood room,
stirring the large vat of gingerbread
batter, and feeding her brother plate
after plate of sweet food. What once
Hansel had dreamt of, now he dreaded:
cakes laden with cream, bowls of candy, and iced gingerbread.

"Getting fatter, soon to batter," the witch repeated each
morning as she inspected Hansel to see how his plumping had
progressed. Unable to see properly, she'd pull out his finger and
feel it. "Too skinny! More food!" she'd cackle. "Once you're
fat enough, I'll batter you up and bake you into a gingerbread
boy for my dinner."

"No!" cried Gretel this particular morning.

"Disobey me and your brother will die sooner," hissed the
witch. "Do as I say and you'll have more time together."

"Time," said Hansel to himself, furrowing his brow.

"Gretel," he whispered that night as she fed him cream cakes, "when you're in the wood room, fetch me the thinnest stick you can find."

"Yes, brother," said Gretel, realizing her brother had a plan. And the children smiled at each other, put their thumbs together, and nodded.

Gretel slipped Hansel a thin stick, and the next morning he presented that to the witch rather than his finger, which indeed was getting plumper.

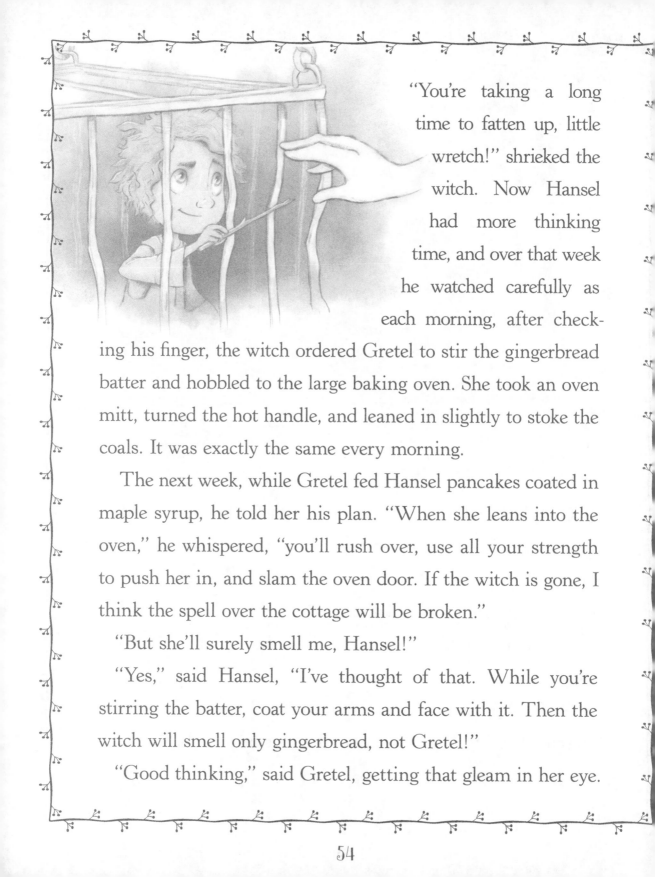

"You're taking a long time to fatten up, little wretch!" shrieked the witch. Now Hansel had more thinking time, and over that week he watched carefully as each morning, after checking his finger, the witch ordered Gretel to stir the gingerbread batter and hobbled to the large baking oven. She took an oven mitt, turned the hot handle, and leaned in slightly to stoke the coals. It was exactly the same every morning.

The next week, while Gretel fed Hansel pancakes coated in maple syrup, he told her his plan. "When she leans into the oven," he whispered, "you'll rush over, use all your strength to push her in, and slam the oven door. If the witch is gone, I think the spell over the cottage will be broken."

"But she'll surely smell me, Hansel!"

"Yes," said Hansel, "I've thought of that. While you're stirring the batter, coat your arms and face with it. Then the witch will smell only gingerbread, not Gretel!"

"Good thinking," said Gretel, getting that gleam in her eye.

"But, Gretel," said Hansel, "you will have to be quick."

"I can do that," said Gretel.

"And you will have to be strong."

"I can do that, too," said Gretel.

"And you will have to be brave."

Hansel saw his sister's lip quiver.

"You can do that, Gretel," he said.

Gretel smiled, and they put their thumbs together and nodded.

The next morning, it happened just as Hansel had foretold. The witch checked Hansel's finger and crossly ordered Gretel to stir the batter. She then hobbled to the fire, leaned into the oven, and began stoking the coals.

Gretel moved like lightning. The witch's nose didn't even twitch; she never knew Gretel was coming. Gretel pushed the evil witch into the oven and, although the handle was scalding hot on her hand, slammed the door shut behind her.

The moment the door locked shut, the bars of Hansel's cage fell to the ground. The witch's spell had been broken.

"You did it, Gretel!" cried Hansel.

"We did it, Hansel!" cried Gretel.

The children hugged.

"What shall we do now, brother?" asked Gretel.

"I think I have a plan," said Hansel.

"Of course you do," said Gretel, hugging her dear brother again. "Tell me all about it."

5.

THE DEATH OF the witch had also broken the famine that blighted the land. The ground was softened by cleansing rains, and by spring, crops flourished and food was plentiful.

Hansel and Gretel lived in the cottage, no longer made of gingerbread but a strong and sturdy brick. They'd strung a large banner above the door: H&G SWEET THINGS EMPORIUM AND INVENTIONS WORKSHOP.

The emporium sold all sort of candy and gingerbreads and a few other things Hansel had created in his workshop—

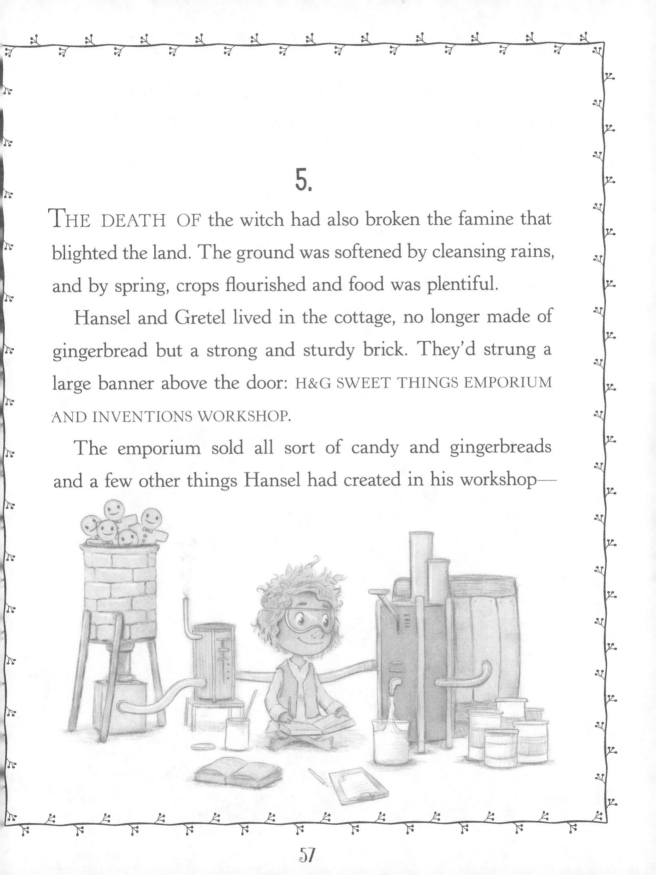

including his first invention, the Gingerbread Batter Burn Balm, a soothing cream that had healed Gretel's hand.

The vegetable patch now burst with an abundance of strawberries and grapes, pumpkins, corn, beans, and broccoli, and Hansel, who had rather lost his sweet tooth, would crunch on cucumbers morning to night.

People came from all over to try the mouthwatering sweets and salads, paying as little or as much as they could afford. Everyone lived happily ever after—and nobody's stomach ever grumbled again.

THE EMPEROR'S NEW CLOTHES

1.

ONCE UPON A TIME, in a faraway land, lived a young man called Christian, who served in the palace of a wealthy emperor, enjoying the privileges of court life. Christian valued his place at court, for he'd once been very poor and knew the terrible feeling of cold when one didn't have enough clothes, and hunger when there wasn't enough food.

Some years earlier, when Christian had been a young boy, he and his shepherd father had been tending their flock in the hills outside the palace walls when they'd come across a boy, around the same age as Christian, encircled by wolves.

Unbeknown to them, this boy was the emperor's son, and he'd disobediently left the palace without his guard, chasing

a beautiful peacock. Enchanted by the colorful plumage, the boy was deaf to the hungry wolves' howls. Christian watched in awe as his father approached the snarling wolves, enduring their savage scratches as he beat them away from the boy, lunging at them with his crook.

"No!" yelled the father with a final lunge at the last wolf. As the wolf retreated, the young boy looked up as if awoken from a trance, only at that moment seeing the danger he'd been in.

"Thank you," he said.

Christian asked, "Why did you risk your life, Father? You don't know that boy."

"We are shepherds, my son—protectors," replied his father. "We should do what's right, even if it's dangerous."

The emperor was so grateful for the safe return of his son that he rewarded Christian's father, who became the young prince's royal protector. Christian became his royal companion. The two boys grew up together, playing as friends, although Christian knew his place with this boy who would become emperor.

As they got older, Christian became very good at entertaining, and the prince became very good at being entertained.

When both their fathers died, the prince became the emperor and Christian became the royal protector. Secretly, both young men worried that they wouldn't fill their fathers' shoes. Christian worked hard to become strong and fit, so he'd be ready should there be an attack on the emperor. Meanwhile, the emperor worked hard to ensure he looked like an emperor—for sadly, too easily enchanted by beautiful gifts and the flattery of the courtiers, he'd grown into a vain young man. He loved clothes and would spend hours dressing to impress, in suits made from only the finest, the rarest, the most exquisitely colored fabrics the royal suit-makers could find.

The emperor had suits made for every occasion and every imperial task. He had suits for eating breakfast, suits for riding, suits for playing croquet, suits for listening to amusing

stories (which Christian was very good at telling), suits for feeding the imperial peacocks, even suits for inspecting the royal suit collection. Indeed, the young emperor spent much time planning his next suit and little time planning for the care of his subjects and kingdom. Christian attended to the emperor during all his activities. A gifted sportsman and a charming and good-humored companion, he was a much-liked member of the court. "That Christian," the other courtiers would say, "you can count on him to brighten things up. Always ready with a story, guaranteed to put a smile on the emperor's face!"

One day Christian and the emperor were out riding in the hills (the emperor wearing a jaunty golden suit with small horseshoe motifs embroidered in fine silken thread at the cuffs) when they rode past some villagers collecting juniper berries. The emperor, who had little contact with life outside the palace walls, was taken aback by their appearance.

"Why are their clothes so dirty?" he exclaimed. "And why such drab colors?"

"They only have one set of clothes each," explained Christian, who sometimes wished his emperor would spend a little more time out in his kingdom.

"Well, that's ridiculous!" declared the emperor.

"Perhaps if the Royal Treasury helped the villagers more, Your Highness . . . ," offered Christian.

"Oh, don't bore me. You're supposed to protect me from such things. Come, Christian, let's away. I need to change into my luncheon suit."

Christian sighed as he turned his horse back toward the palace. But it wasn't his place to instruct the emperor, and he didn't want to upset anyone—he loved his life at the palace, and he wanted to keep things that way. He knew the emperor was a little vain, but, Christian reasoned, he was still growing into his job. Christian wanted to protect the emperor, just like his father had—but he had yet to learn that wolves didn't always look like wolves.

2.

ONE DAY, as the emperor sat on his throne wearing his throne-sitting suit, the prime minister suggested an imperial tour of the villages beyond the palace. The villagers were starting to grumble that the new emperor cared only for palace life and not for them. The visit would show them the emperor was a caring leader.

The emperor leaped at the idea—sadly for the wrong reasons. "Indeed!" he cried, clapping his hands. "I must have a kingdom-touring suit made! Call for the finest fabrics!"

The royal call went out and was heard by two swindlers passing through the kingdom. They came to the court and were presented to the emperor.

Christian watched them bow a little too low before the throne.

"Your Royal Highness," they said together, "we offer our services as weavers and tailors, of the finest of cloths, in the most exquisite of colors . . . and with an extra, *special* quality—a divining quality, if you will."

That got the emperor's attention. "What kind of divining quality?" he asked, leaning closer.

"The best sort, sire," said one of the swindlers. "Our fabrics are able to be seen only by people of wisdom. Anyone stupid and unfit to hold their office will be unable to see the cloth, and the suit from which it is made. An invaluable thing for an emperor, don't you agree?"

The emperor did agree, as the swindlers knew he would. Their plan was devious but quite ingenious: they knew everyone would claim they could see the cloth, to protect their reputations and positions. The swindlers could collect a rich payment in gold by simply pretending to weave a cloth and make a suit that never existed.

"Imagine, sire!" said the other swindler. "Not only will you look magnificent, but you'll know who is stupid and who is wise. And no one in the world but you will have such a suit."

Christian wondered how such a thing could be possible, but the emperor was, again, enchanted. "I must have this suit!" he declared.

"It will not come cheap, though, sire," warned the swindlers. "It will take much gold and many reels of fine silks."

"Pay these weavers what they ask," the emperor instructed the royal treasurer. "Give them whatever they request, and have them start immediately."

The treasurer looked hesitant but gave the devious weavers a loom, a sewing machine, and reels of precious threads, and they set upon their task with zeal.

They hid the threads, yet dashed around the loom with their arms stretched out, as if pulling silks and threading yarn. Their knees wobbled as if buckling from carrying heavy bolts of fabric, and they worked day and night, very busily doing nothing at all.

The emperor was impressed with the weavers' dedication but grew impatient to see their work.

"I will inspect their progress," he said. But then he remembered the weavers saying anyone unfit for their office wouldn't see the cloth, and he felt unsure. What if he, the emperor himself, couldn't see it? He was still new as emperor and sometimes worried he wouldn't live up to the standard his father had set.

I'll send my prime minister, he decided. *He is the wisest of men and will certainly be able to see my cloth.*

And so the prime minister was summoned. "Visit the weavers," the emperor instructed. "I should like to know how they're getting on."

"Yes, Your Highness," said the prime minister, although he too was a little fearful he might not see anything. And, indeed, when he walked into the room, he saw the two weavers busily 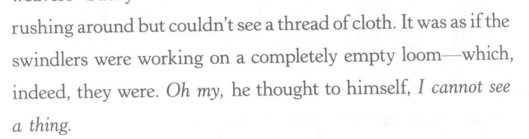 rushing around but couldn't see a thread of cloth. It was as if the swindlers were working on a completely empty loom—which, indeed, they were. *Oh my,* he thought to himself, *I cannot see a thing.*

The swindlers, sensing the prime minister's reluctance, approached him, bowing low.

"What do you think, Prime Minister?" one asked. "Will the emperor appreciate this exquisite pattern? Do you not think the colors will match his royal complexion perfectly?"

The prime minister cocked his head one way, then the other. He squinted and strained his eyes, but he could see nothing.

"Tell us, prime minister," said the other swindler. "For surely you can see it? Surely you, the emperor's most trusted minister, can see our work?"

But the prime minister could not.

Am I stupid? he thought. *I wouldn't have thought it so. This mustn't be known—I cannot lose my position.*

And so he cleared his throat and declared the cloth the most beautiful and intricately woven he'd ever seen.

"What do you think will please the emperor about it most?" pressed the swindlers.

The prime minister coughed. "The brilliant gold trim," he declared, looking out the window.

"Oh, yes, an excellent choice. What taste and discrimination you have," they replied. "And please, wise prime minister, order us more silk and gold thread so we can make it even more beautiful."

The prime minister had no choice but to comply. He left the room and reported to the emperor that the weavers were making a cloth of unimaginable beauty.

A few days later, the emperor sent his royal treasurer to ask when the suit would be ready. Like the prime minister, the treasurer could see nothing on the swindlers' loom, but was too afraid to say so.

The prime minister could see it, she thought, *yet I cannot. I must be unfit for office, but I have six children to feed and mustn't lose my position at court.*

And so the royal treasurer also declared the cloth the finest she'd seen. "The prime minister didn't adequately convey the beauty!" she exclaimed. "The vibrancy, the richness!"

"We're so pleased you like it," said one of the swindlers, barely able to conceal a smirk. "Which aspect do you think will most enchant His Royal Highness?"

"Ah, well . . . I'd say the intricate images—the ah, er . . ."

"Yes, royal treasurer, which image?"

"Do you mean the peacock?" asked the other swindler, gesturing to the empty space in the middle of the loom.

"Ah, yes! The peacock, the emperor's favorite bird! And with such detailing. Exquisite!"

The royal treasurer reported that the cloth was indeed magnificent, and soon everyone at court was talking about how grand the emperor's new clothes were going to be.

The emperor could think of nothing else. "Tell me again, prime minister, about my new suit," he said the next day in the throne room. He was wearing his

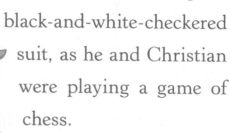

black-and-white-checkered suit, as he and Christian were playing a game of chess.

"Oh, the silver—" began the prime minister.

"I thought you said it was gold," said Christian.

"Did I say silver? I meant gold. The most luminous gold!" exclaimed the prime minister, a little too enthusiastically.

"And the eagle!" added the royal treasurer.

"Not peacock?" asked the emperor. "I thought you said peacock."

"Yes, quite right," said the royal treasurer quickly. "A magnificent peacock."

"Christian," said the emperor, feeling a little impatient with his ministers, "will you please go and inspect my suit?"

"Of course, sire," replied Christian. He bowed to the emperor and left for the weaving room.

When he arrived, as had happened with the prime minister and royal treasurer before him, Christian saw nothing on the loom. He watched as the two devious weavers rushed around, gesturing frantically at thin air.

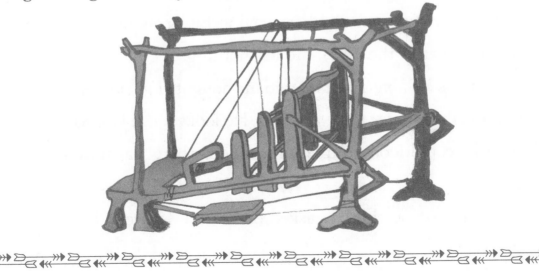

Panicking a little, Christian went closer. *Is there something I can't see?* he asked himself. *Could the fabric truly have powers to tell the wise from the stupid?* He stepped closer still.

"No farther, please," cried one of the weavers. "The fabric is quite fragile."

But Christian ignored her, waving his arms up and down in the center of the loom. He felt nothing.

There is nothing here, Christian thought. *I'm sure of it. No gold or silver, no peacock or eagle.* He looked and looked again, until he could look no more, for indeed there was nothing to look at!

"What do you think?" asked one of the weavers, her voice

wavering. "What part of the emperor's new cloth do you admire the most?"

Christian said nothing.

"You can see it, can't you?" said the other swindler. "It is true, of course, that the cloth cannot be seen by stupid people, but surely you, sir, the emperor's royal protector, can see it?"

Christian left the room without a word.

These people are tricksters, he said to himself. *But why did the prime minister and royal treasurer say they saw something? Then Christian had a terrible thought. What will happen if the emperor falls for this trick too? What if he goes out into the villages wearing only his underwear?*

Christian imagined the royal procession: the trumpeters and banner-bearers marching in front; the royal guards in their uniforms bringing up the rear; and, in the middle, the emperor, the center of attention, wearing only his underpants.

He'd look ridiculous, Christian realized. *He'd die of embarrassment! Everyone would laugh. But the prime minister and royal treasurer must have told him they could see the suit so no one would think them stupid.*

Then Christian had another terrible thought, this time for himself.

If I tell the emperor the truth, perhaps everyone will think I'm stupid. Maybe no one will believe me over the prime minister and royal treasurer. And what will they do? They might call me a liar, to protect themselves; they could even have me thrown into the royal dungeon!

Maybe, he reasoned, *it's best for me to say nothing, keep out of the way. It's not really my responsibility.* But that didn't feel good to him either. Something about it niggled at his head and his heart. Christian could almost hear his father's voice echo through his mind: *Do what's right.* But Christian, like the prime minister and the royal treasurer, was afraid he'd lose everything if he did.

3.

CHRISTIAN AVOIDED THE EMPEROR, and to his relief, the very next day, the weavers announced the suit was ready for the emperor's approval.

Now it's up to him, Christian thought. *He's the emperor. Surely he'll see there's nothing there and not be afraid to say it.*

The emperor entered the weaving room, flanked by attendants and courtiers.

"Your Royal Highness," said the weavers, swooping down into the lowest of bows. "We are honored. Tell us, sire, how do you like your royal suit, on which we have labored these past days and nights?"

"Is it not magnificent?" said the prime minister.

"Is it not perfect?" said the royal treasurer.

All the other attendants were squinting. The weavers waltzed around the room. "Do you all see?" they cried. "Surely, Your Highness, you have no idiots in your court!"

With that, all those other attendants of the court began to exclaim how beautiful they found the cloth.

"Exquisite!"

"The detail!"

"The colors!"

No one would admit they could see nothing at all. Christian's heart sank. He turned to the emperor. "Sire, what do you see?"

I see nothing, thought the emperor. *Not one thread. Am I unfit to be emperor? Everyone will realize I can't live up to my father.*

The emperor didn't look at Christian. Instead, he turned to the weavers. "Magnificent," he declared. "I'll wear it tomorrow."

"But Your Highness—" Christian started.

"Can you not see the suit?" asked one of the swindlers sharply.

"Well, boy?" snapped the prime minister, who'd always been a bit jealous of Christian's closeness to the emperor. "Can you? To the dungeon with you if you can't, for that surely means you're unfit to serve our royal emperor."

Christian was silent. He wanted to say something, but nothing came out.

The prime minister gave a scoffing laugh and ordered the weavers to have the suit completed by morning for the tour. The emperor glanced at Christian, but then turned toward his attendants, who were encircling him now, crooning, congratulating him on his splendid new suit. Christian left the room unnoticed.

What do I do? he asked himself. *I'm just one voice. Everyone's saying they can see beautiful cloth, but there's nothing there, I know it. And if the emperor insists on wearing this nothing, he'll walk out of the palace gates tomorrow in only his underwear and be eaten alive by the mocking crowd.*

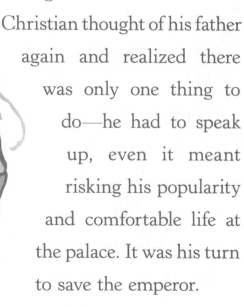

Christian thought of his father again and realized there was only one thing to do—he had to speak up, even it meant risking his popularity and comfortable life at the palace. It was his turn to save the emperor.

4.

THE NEXT MORNING the weavers declared the suit ready and the emperor, attended by the royal dresser, entered the weaving room. Some time later he came out wearing only his underpants: large, baggy, blue-and-white-striped bloomers.

He looks ridiculous! thought Christian. *Why is he doing this? He's the emperor—surely he's not afraid of what others might think?*

The attendants, the guards, the trumpeters, and the banner-bearers were all staring at the emperor. First there was silence. Then, as they realized their jobs would be in danger if they laughed, all began to cheer: "Bravo, Your Majesty, bravo!"

"This is crazy," said Christian, and he moved toward the emperor.

The prime minister, who'd heard him, blocked his path. "Anyone who doesn't agree the emperor looks the finest he's ever looked will be thrown into the royal dungeon," he stated.

Christian's heart raced, but he knew what he had to do. "Stop!" he cried. Everyone looked at him. "Sire, there is no suit. You're wearing only your underwear, and if you—"

"Hah!" shouted the prime minister furiously. "The shepherd boy can't see the suit. He's unfit. I always thought so. Trust me, sire!"

Christian looked imploringly at the emperor. "Sire, don't go out of the palace grounds like this. Your subjects will surely laugh at you."

The emperor looked at Christian, then down at himself. He seemed not to see his skinny legs poking out from his blue-and-white-striped underpants.

"Sire," said the royal treasurer, terrified now that the emperor would know she'd lied, "trust us, not this shepherd boy."

"Guards," cried the prime minister, pointing at Christian, "take him to the dungeon. He is stripped of all title and privileges."

Two guards roughly took hold of Christian, who watched helplessly as the near-naked emperor walked toward the huge palace gates, which were being slowly wound open. Once the gates had fully opened, all the villagers beyond would see him.

There was no time to lose. With a roar, Christian broke free of the guards. He ripped the prime minister's cape from his shoulders and rushed toward the emperor, shouting, "No!" as he lunged and covered him with it just seconds before the gates opened wide.

The emperor looked at Christian as if awoken from a trance, only at that moment seeing the danger he'd been in.

"Christian," he said, "I'm in my underpants! The people could have seen me like this. Me, the emperor! You've saved me from such embarrassment!"

"It was my pleasure, Your Royal Highness," replied Christian.

In gratitude for his boldness and courage, the emperor declared that Christian would now be both royal protector and advisor. He then glared at the prime minister and royal treasurer who, quite sensibly, looked very worried.

The hidden spools of thread were discovered, and the swindlers were caught and thrown into the royal dungeon. The prime minister and royal treasurer now had to seek Christian's approval on all matters of court. And the first matter was the distribution of many of the emperor's old clothes throughout the kingdom.

And they all—well, mostly all—lived happily ever after.

PRINCE LEO AND THE SLEEPING PRINCESS

1.

ONCE UPON A TIME, in a faraway kingdom, lived a young prince. Prince Leopold Charming, Leo to his friends, was a prince from a long line of princes who, throughout the centuries, had fulfilled the Charming family's time-honored role of rescuing damsels, mostly princesses, in distress.

Leo showed every indication that he would uphold the Charming family tradition brilliantly: he was strong and athletic, an expert horseman and archer, and a quite superb fencer, and he practiced all with great diligence. He was less interested in ballroom dancing, which was often part of the post-rescue work, but as he was an obedient boy he persevered with his waltz and was, according to the royal dance master, really quite good, with a strong sense of rhythm. Leo was also a disciplined student of princely history, reading the Charming Family Chronicles and learning from both the triumphs and travails of his ancestors' rescues.

The great hall of Charming Castle was filled with paintings in heavy gold frames displaying family portraits of princes and the princesses they had rescued and married: Leo's parents, grandparents, great-grandparents, great-great-grandparents, and even-greater-grandparents. Leo didn't mind princesses—

he knew quite a few nice ones—but he didn't want to get married, at least not now, at least not for ages.

For Leo had a lot to do. He played the violin, both alone and with his friends, and he was particularly good at royal tennis: his princely brain was highly mathematical, and he loved to calculate exactly where the ball would land if he hit it at a certain angle and speed. Leo couldn't spend as much time as he'd like playing, though, for he had his daily fencing and archery practice, his tower-scaling and castle-entwining-briar-beating, and most importantly, his dragon-slaying drills to complete.

Leo didn't mind all the training—he understood it was his duty—but he did sometimes wonder why damsel deliverance always came down to the princes. His closest friends, the Honorable Viscounts Edvard and Gilbert, would both make admirable defenders, but they were never called—it was always the princes. And, Leo wondered, what about the princesses? Could they never rescue themselves?

Leo raised this with his father one day as they walked in the royal gardens training their falcons, their dogs obediently by their sides.

"Now there's a thought," said King Oskar, pondering the question as he tethered the peregrine falcon that had just returned to

his arm. "Do you know, Leo, I've never thought of that—it's never come up. I like your thinking, though."

That made Leo smile: he liked to make his father happy.

"I suppose it's about our role," continued the king. "The viscounts—and those dukes and marquises—all have their roles to play, and we ours. We have this wonderful palace, these beautiful gardens . . ."

"And the royal tennis court," chipped in Leo.

"Indeed," said his father, smiling, for the king knew how much his son loved his royal tennis. "And with those privileges come responsibilities. Our responsibility is to serve when needed, by rescuing—it's what we do, and we must ensure we do it well. Let's walk some more, Leo."

The king and the prince walked down the ordered paths of the palace's highly ornamental parterre gardens: straight gravel-filled paths separated by square garden beds, all exactly the same size and bordered by green box-hedging, bursting with snowdrops, hyacinths, geraniums, lavender, and precisely placed and masterfully pruned rosebushes. The garden had been first planned and planted by Leo's great-great-great-grandfather and grandmother and had been immaculately maintained ever since. In the exact center was a pond, and in the middle of the pond was an imposing bronze statue of Prince Leo's great-great-great-grandfather, slaying a dragon.

While Leo loved a fast gallop in the woods outside the palace walls, rushing at breakneck speed, he also loved walking in the palace gardens. It made him feel calm and secure—as if things were under control, at peace. It was a good place for thinking, his father often said, which was why he would often walk there with Leo to instruct him in the Charming family ways. And so it was this day, when the king told Leo the legend of the sleeping princess.

2.

"LEGEND HAS IT," began the king, "that there was once a small kingdom neighboring ours, ruled by a gracious king and queen, who after many years of waiting and wishing had a daughter, whom they named Aurora. There was much rejoicing throughout the land, and in honor of the Princess Aurora's christening, a royal banquet was held. The king and queen invited all the fairies in the kingdom except one, an evil fairy, for they feared she would ruin the celebration."

"Why do I get the feeling that wasn't a good idea?" asked Leo.

"Quite," said the king. "And, indeed, when all but one of the good fairies had bestowed their blessings on the little princess,

a black raven flew through the palace window and transformed into the evil fairy. Outraged that she'd been excluded, she put a curse on the princess, declaring that when she was sixteen years of age, she would prick her finger on a spindle and die."

"Prick her finger? That's a bit lame, isn't it, Father?" asked Leo.

"Well, fairies do as fairies do, I suppose," said the king. "Shall I continue?"

"Yes, Father," said Prince Leo, although he wasn't completely sure what this story had to do with him.

"The queen and king were devastated they would soon lose their so-longed-for daughter. There was, however, one fairy left to bestow a final blessing, and while she couldn't cancel the evil fairy's curse—"

"Why not?" asked Leo.

"Well, because once some things are said, they can't be unsaid," replied the king, "but the last fairy could soften the curse so the princess wouldn't die, but rather would fall into a deep sleep. The good fairy pronounced her blessing, and the evil fairy hissed, transformed into a snake, and slipped out of the palace before anyone could catch her. The king ordered every spindle in the land to be burned. He made it a crime punishable by death to spin anything anywhere in the kingdom, yet somehow, on her sixteenth birthday—"

"Sixteen, same age as me," said Leo.

"Yes, an important age for princes and princesses," said the king. "Well, on her sixteenth birthday, the princess wandered into a room in the castle where an old servant-woman in a black cape was hunched over a spindle, spinning thread through her gnarled fingers. The old woman was—"

"I know!" shouted Leo, for he was well versed in the ways of evil fairies and goblins. "The old woman was the evil fairy in disguise!"

"Yes," said the king, looking proud. "Well done, Leo."

Leo beamed as his father continued.

"The old woman beckoned to Princess Aurora. "Come in, my dear. Let me show you the fine gold thread I'm spinning," she croaked. The princess, who'd of course never seen a spindle before, was entranced. The woman handed her the spindle, on which Aurora pricked her finger. In that instant, she fell to the ground."

"But not dead, right?" said Leo. "Just sleeping, because of the good fairy's counter-blessing?"

"Exactly," said King Oskar. "Seconds later, a chambermaid walked in and found the princess lying on the floor and a large black spider scuttling away. She called for the king and queen, and they called for the court doctors and the good fairies, but no one could wake the princess. The curse had taken hold. Aurora was carried to a room high in a tower and surrounded by garlands of flowers. Her royal flag flew from the tower, but inside, the princess lay completely still."

"That's sad," said Leo.

"Yes, terribly," said the king. "Everyone was so sad that the king and queen asked a good fairy to cast a spell of sleep over the whole castle. Everyone who lived in the castle—the cooks, the servants, the footmen and ladies-in-waiting, knights and ministers and even the king and queen—all fell into a deep sleep exactly where they were."

"That's a bit creepy," said Leo.

"Yes, I suppose it is," said King Oskar with a shudder. "The whole castle was now wrapped in timeless sleep. Years went by, and the trees in the grounds grew tall, the bushes thick, the grass high. Thorny briars curled up the walls and turrets. It is said that all this happened over a hundred years ago, and that the forgotten palace sleeps on to this day."

"Would anything awaken the princess?"

"According to legend, 'only the piercing of the evil fairy's heart by a king's son, one young and true, bold and of blood royally blue' can break the spell," said the king.

Now Leo understood why his father was telling him the story. "And that's where we come in, isn't it?" said Leo.

"Where you come in, maybe," replied the king. "My princess-saving days are over, but this is what you've been training for, Leo. Always take your shield and sword when you ride in the woods, and ride farther and deeper in—perhaps you'll find the hidden castle."

Leo obeyed his father. Every week he'd mount his white stallion and dutifully ride out in the woods, careful to take a different path each time, his sword and shield (royal-blue-colored) always with him. But the weeks went by and Leo never saw anything, which was, frankly, disappointing: he'd been excited at the thought of putting his training to the test, but there seemed no princess with whom to do it. He began to think the legend of the sleeping princess was just a story after all.

3.

SOME MONTHS LATER Leo was dutifully setting off for his weekly ride into the woods when Viscount Edvard called, "Leo, stay here. Play royal tennis with us instead!"

"I can't," said Leo, strapping his sword to his back. "It's time for my woods ride."

"But you never find anything, Leo!" said Viscount Gilbert.

It was true: despite his many rides, he never did find anything. Leo was sorely tempted to stay, but he knew his duty. "Maybe later," he said, and climbed onto his horse.

"Royal tennis will be more fun," pleaded Viscount Edvard. But it was too late: Leo had ridden down the path, out the royal gates, and into the woods.

Heading westward, Leo rode for over an hour through particularly dense forest before he came to a thick tangle of thorny briars. "Just like in the story," he said to himself.

Right, left, right, left. Leo moved his
swordexpertly through the tangle
of thorns, grateful for
all his lessons and arm-
strengthening exercises.

Just as he was tiring, his
sword ripped through the last cluster and
Leo saw what it had been hiding—two gatehouses
to the sides of a long and narrow stone bridge, which spanned
a deep, tree-filled ravine and led to an imposing castle.

Leo climbed off his horse and led it as he approached the bridge, his whole body tingling with excitement. He slashed at the thorny creepers covering the door of a gatehouse and pushed with all his strength to open it. Inside he found two armor-clad guards, crossbows still in hand, slumped on the floor. He checked their chests. They were still breathing: they were asleep. Leo looked up at the castle. The tallest tower, entwined in brambles, flew a tattered royal flag.

It hadn't been just a story! Leo had found the castle of the sleeping princess.

Leo looked up the castle's wall, calculating the height of the tower. *Shouldn't take too long,* he thought as he approached it and grabbed hold of the thorny branches, his hands protected by his thick riding gloves, then began to climb.

But as he reached the top, a black raven swooped at him, pecking viciously at his hands. It swooped again and Leo swung at it, using his tennis backhand stroke to send it tumbling away. Leo pulled himself up onto the stone window ledge and looked in. There on a bed, surrounded by dry, dead flowers, was a girl in a blue dress. Leo couldn't help but also notice a cello and a royal tennis racquet leaning against the wall. "It really is the princess!" he exclaimed. "How terrible! All the things she could have been doing. I must break the curse."

Just then the raven returned, pecking at his eyes. Leo swiped at it again, but this time he lost his grip on the brambles and fell from the ledge as the

raven swooped back up into the sky. Luckily he managed to grab hold of some brambles and break his fall just before he hit the bottom.

"That was close!" he said. "Now I need to find that evil fairy. Perhaps if I can get inside the castle . . ."

But then there was a ferocious crack of thunder from the sky, and although it was the middle of the day, everything went dark.

Leo's horse whinnied nervously and he jumped onto its back, a tremor of nerves shooting through his body. What would happen next? Leo didn't have to wait long to find out.

"Who dares disturb my accursed castle?" shrieked a voice.

Leo looked up to see a figure, taller than three women and dressed in a swirling purple-and-black winged cape, with a horned crown on her head, standing on top of the castle's highest turret. She held a long scepter, which she now pointed at Leo.

"The evil fairy. Yes!" said Leo.

The fairy grew
taller still, and now
there was a flash of lightning.

The thorny briars clutching the castle walls sprang out, as if alive, and curled toward Leo on the bridge. Leo again took up his sword, and he struck at them powerfully, sending them flying to either side of him.

The fairy, enraged, raised her scepter again and sent showers of fire down onto the bridge, igniting the brambles.

Flames began to lick around Leo's boots, but the prince stood his ground, using his shield to deflect the fiery darts the evil one rained down upon him and his horse.

Now the trees in the ravine caught fire, and the enchantress raised her scepter again, unleashing a lightning bolt that struck the

bridge in front of Leo right between him and the castle, the stone crumbling into the flames below.

"You will not proceed!" the enchantress bellowed. "My curse will stand. You will concede!"

Prince Leo knew he wouldn't concede. Everything he'd trained for had prepared him for this moment.

"That's not the way we do things in my family," he said as he prodded his horse firmly, backtracked a little, and then charged toward

the breach in the bridge. With a flying leap, he landed on the other side.

The enchantress, incensed, transformed into a huge black-and-purple dragon, spraying a hideous green slime from its mouth and hurling fireballs from its claws. The dragon swept down and landed beside Leo. It belched a torrent of green slime

at him, but he used his shield and held strong, deflecting it. The slime hit the castle wall, blasting through the stone.

That was close, thought Leo.

The dragon struck again and again, but each time Leo matched it perfectly, until, repelling a giant fireball and sending it scorching into the dragon, Leo lost his footing. He scrambled up but struggled to get back into position in time to deflect the next slime attack—Leo knew the moment it hit his shield that he'd made a mistake. The shield flew out of his hand.

The dragon moved in. Leo held his sword tight and advanced.

He remembered what his father had told him of the legend: "Only the piercing of the evil fairy's heart by a king's son, one young and true, bold and of blood royally blue can break the spell."

I'm a king's son, he told himself. *This is what I need to do, what I have trained for. Pierce the heart, break the curse, and let that princess get on with what she needs to do.*

Leo took a deep breath. He knew he had to get close. He advanced on the dragon, ducking the slime and fireballs, until he was so close he could see its hideous scaly skin. The dragon rose up on its hind legs, exposing its chest.

Now! thought Leo.

He hurled his sword, and it pierced the dragon's heart.

YEWARRRRRRRRRGGHHHHH!

The dragon's scream was earsplitting. It lurched and then fell from the bridge, into the fiery pit below. There was an explosion and then, eerily, nothing. At that moment, the sky became a brilliant blue and the sun shone its rays all over the castle. Leo's sword lay glistening on the bridge by the castle gates, which now opened before him.

Wait until I tell Father about this! Leo thought.

4.

LEO WALKED THROUGH the castle gates just as guards in the courtyard got up from the ground, stretching. A doorman held the castle door open for Leo, stifling a yawn, and inside the great entrance hall, servants, footmen, and ladies-in-waiting rose to their feet too, looking bewildered.

"Um, I need to see the princess," Leo told a young woman who was rubbing her eyes.

"The princess!" she exclaimed, as if suddenly remembering. "Have you not heard, sir, that my lady is asleep, victim of the cruelest of curses? She'll be asleep for years, until a king's son, someone young—"

She stopped mid-sentence, looking intently at Leo.

"You! Are you the one who is young and true, bold and of blood royally blue?"

"Well, madam, I am royal," replied Leo. "And, if I may say so, I think I have just been pretty bold with a particularly evil fairy."

"And she is dead?" asked the lady-in-waiting.

"Very much so," confirmed Leo.

"Then the spell is broken, and Princess Aurora will be awake! Oh my goodness, I must go to her! And the king and queen!"

The lady-in-waiting turned to a footman. "Call for the bells to be rung and trumpets sounded. The spell over this castle is broken! And look, on the stairs!"

The lady-in-waiting dropped to the floor in a low curtsy. Leo looked up to the top of the grand staircase to see the princess awake and smiling, standing in between a king and queen (Leo could tell them by their crowns).

As the bells rang out
and the royal trumpeters began
to play, all the servants bowed low.

"Your Majesties!" Prince Leo bowed down
in front of the king, queen, and Princess Aurora.

"Arise, noble prince," said the queen. "With your courage,
you have destroyed the evil fairy and broken the curse. What
is your name?"

"Prince Leopold Charming at your service," replied Leo,
grinning.

"We owe you an enormous debt of gratitude," said the queen.
"I could kiss you, I'm so happy! May I?"

"Of course," replied Leo happily, "but you don't owe me
anything, Your Majesty. It's my job."

"Well, we can still say thank you!" said Princess Aurora,
descending the stairs. "I can't tell you how happy I am to be
awake. I have a lot to do! I can get on with my archery and—"

"Archery?" asked Leo. He wasn't expecting that.

"Oh yes," said the king, looking proudly at his daughter. "Aurora has a great eye. She's quite the expert markswoman."

"And then there's her tennis," said the queen. "That volley! Ah, and now you'll play again, my dear girl."

"I adore tennis," said Leo. "We have a really good court at our castle. I play with my two best friends, Edvard and Gilbert, and we'd love another player for doubles. You could come over and play with us one day, if you'd like?"

"I'd be thrilled to," said Aurora. "I'm a little out of practice, though."

Leo grinned. "That will make you easier to beat."

"Not that out of practice," replied Aurora quickly.

"You're on!" said Leo.

Over the next weeks and months, Leo and Aurora spent a lot of time together, playing in their newly formed string quartet with Gilbert and Edvard or on the royal tennis court, where Gilbert and Edvard always wanted to pair up with Aurora, for she was by far the strongest player.

But Leo always had Aurora as his partner.

"After all, guys," said Aurora, "it was Leo who did the dragon-slaying and curse-breaking."

"Quite true," said Edvard.

"Fair point," conceded Gilbert.

And so, more often than not, Leo and Aurora thrashed the viscounts, and they all lived happily ever after.